ENC

A Call to Compassion is a book about a journey to which all of us have been called. It will no doubt help men and women alike, as Michal Ann and James have brought wonderful insights, moving personal testimonies, and stories about our heroes of the faith who embraced the same journey. This priceless couple has once again brought us a gem that will help us come into the fullness of Christ.

—Bill Johnson
Author of *When Heaven Invades Earth*
and other books

A Call to Compassion, along with the other books in the Women on the Frontlines series, is full of encouragement, exhortation, and compassion for women who are struggling to become the women of destiny God has created them to be. Michal Ann poured out her heart in a vulnerable, even tender way to her fellow sisters in Christ. It is almost as if she is God's cheerleader for the reader even to this day, exhorting them, "Go on, Sister, you can do it!" It is my honor, along with my husband, Mike, to continue to walk with James now that Michal Ann has graduated to her heavenly reward. So, come on now, pick up the baton! Let love take action in your life and make a difference for Jesus Christ's sake!

—*Cindy Jacobs*
Generals International
Red Oak, Texas

With a balanced presentation, Michal Ann and James challenge women and men both to fulfill their potential in God without compromise. I have known this family well for years and had the pleasure of serving on their Encounters Network board of directors. They have lived their message well. In the Women on the Frontlines series, this "Female Hall of Fame" of courage, intimacy, and compassion will especially inspire our younger sisters, who have so few heroes and heroines to look up to as examples.

—*Elizabeth Alves*
Founder of Increase International
Author of *Mighty Prayer Warrior* and other books

This dear couple has exemplified godly living with a prophetic edge, prayerful actions, and an unusual partnering that still resounds across the globe to this day. The Holy Spirit chose well when he highlighted this couple to me years ago to extend an invitation for them to move to Music City, USA. I watched them birth the Women on the Frontlines movement. It was a joy to participate in their progression from courage to prayer to compassion. Now it is your turn to be impacted by these compelling writings and carry the torch of Jesus into your generation.

—*Dr. Don Finto*
Pastor Emeritus of Belmont Church
Nashville, Tennessee
Founder of the Caleb Company

I have personally known the Golls for years, and I had the honor of commissioning them as apostolic prophets within our HIM global network. Sue and I cherish our years with them as a couple and cheer James on as he continues to carry the Kingdom message of Jesus around the world. Together they birthed a fresh movement, now stewarded by others, called Women on the Frontlines. I applaud their work together and the distinct lineage and legacy of Michal Ann's life message as expressed in Compassion Acts.

—*Dr. Che Ahn*
Founder of HRock Church and Harvest International Ministries
Chancellor of the Wagner Leadership Institute

I have personally had the honor of knowing James and the late Michal Ann Goll for more than forty years. They served with me in Kansas City for over a decade in various capacities, always demonstrating a lavish love for Jesus. I commend to you these vintage writings in this Women on the Frontlines series of books. The Golls are among those who long to see Jesus receive the rewards for His suffering. I give a hearty *amen* to Michal Ann's lineage and legacy of her ministry and the teachings found in these books.

—*Mike Bickle*
Founder of the IHOP-KC
Author of *Passion for Jesus* and many other books

We loved our years ministering together with Michal Ann and James Goll. Their writings have impacted the global body of Christ. Beautifully, they have called us to take courage, dwell in the secret place, and to let compassionate love take action. These many anecdotes and examples from both the past and the present from those who made a difference in this life call us to follow in their footsteps. Michal Ann used to exhort us to have our own Hall of Heroes. As you read these Women on the Frontlines books, I am sure she will be added to yours. Now it is our turn to answer the call of the Holy Spirit and volunteer freely in the day of His power. Above all, like Michal Ann, let love have the final say.

—*Wesley and Stacey Campbell*
Revival Now! Ministries
Kelowna, British Columbia, Canada

The Salvation Army's founder, William Booth, urged the members of his army to "try tears" when all else fails, because, as Lord Byron once said, "the dew of compassion is a tear!" Sometimes, compassion isn't just a character trait or a spiritual sense within a person, but rather a learned response. I urge you to read this book and *learn compassion!*

—*Steve Shultz*
The Elijah List (www.elijahlist.com)

WOMEN ON THE FRONTLINES

A Call to Compassion

Taking God's Unfailing Love to Your World

James & Michal Ann Goll

BroadStreet
PUBLISHING

BroadStreet Publishing Group, LLC
Racine, Wisconsin, USA
BroadStreetPublishing.com

A Call to Compassion
Taking God's Unfailing Love to Your World

Cover design by Chris Garborg at garborgdesign.com
Interior by Katherine Lloyd at theDESKonline.com

Printed in the United States of America
16 17 18 19 20 5 4 3 2 1

DEDICATION

First and foremost, I (Michal Ann) dedicate this book to Jesus, who comes to us with His heart filled with compassion to fulfill every promise. And I want to dedicate this particular book to my grandmother, Ann Lucinda McCoy, whose prayers kept me on the path, always loving Jesus and living for Him every day—and who also had a dream in her heart, to be a missionary to China. In addition, I dedicate *A Call to Compassion* to the many women who have ventured into closed countries with the Good News and were never heard from again. To the keepers of the flame, the champions of compassion, those who have gone on silently before us, whose stories we will not know until we meet in heaven.

Together with Michal Ann, I (James) dedicate this final book of the Women on the Frontlines series to our four miracle children. Your mom now worships God on the other side, but you know she gave everything she had to bring you forth and you were her joy. Her lineage and legacy are deposited in you, Justin, GraceAnn, Tyler, and Rachel. All of us will meet again someday at the waterside.

CONTENTS

FOREWORD

The world is full of victims: victims of war, poverty, terrorism, sex trafficking, slave labor, abuse, sickness, and disease. Where are these victims? They are everywhere. They could be as visible as your neighbor, coworker, or family member, but they could be as hidden from your sight as a young child chained to a bed in a dark brothel, or a young man abducted and recruited into an army where he is trained and commanded to brutally kill the innocent. They could be desperate mothers weeping in the midst of a famine- and drought-afflicted region, unable to feed their children, or they could be the elderly being taken advantage of and abused behind closed doors. Victims are everywhere, and it is compassion that will motivate and empower us to reach them.

Compassion is the response to the suffering of others that motivates a desire to help. When Jesus was "moved with compassion," the blind saw and those with defiled flesh became clean (see Matthew 20:34 and Mark 1:41). His compassion was both the motivator and the conduit through which God's power flowed to bring transformation in lives.

It was God's compassion for mankind in our sinful estate that motivated Him to give all that He is and all that He has for our redemption. "For God so loved the world, that He gave His only begotten Son, that whoever believes in Him shall not perish, but have eternal life" (John 3:16, NIV).

Oh, what a gift! He did not close His eyes or His heart to our need. We had become victims of the power of sin and we could not help ourselves. We could not change our destined end if we remained in that helpless state. God could have judged and condemned us but He did not. He freely demonstrated heartfelt compassion and love that has transformed us. A divine exchange takes place through the power of His compassion and love so that we are no longer victims but victors in Christ when we receive this glorious gift from His heart.

I remember the first time I visited Bangkok, Thailand. Our ministry had not yet been involved in anti-trafficking, but that night in Bangkok transformed my life and our ministry. Sitting at a table right beside me in a restaurant was a man in his mid-fifties with a young girl he had "bought" for the weekend. She was a sweet Thai girl appearing to be around fifteen to eighteen years of age. She looked very nervous but tried to smile.

Confused emotions erupted in me. I felt so much love and compassion for her but anger toward him. I wanted to "punch his lights out" and rescue her. In the midst of this emotional in-burst, the Lord spoke very tenderly, "Patricia, they are both victims." Suddenly God's compassion was filling me for both of them as I was reminded that our battle is not against flesh and blood but against powers of darkness (see Eph. 6:10–12). Although my emotions remained confused and somewhat helpless, I knew God was giving me a perspective that I had not yet considered.

Over the next few days in Bangkok and Pattaya, I had numerous emotional wrestlings due to similar situations, but in the midst of each of them, compassion from the Lord filled me. As a result of that short-term visit, our ministry launched into a successful and fruitful anti-trafficking outreach assignment through which many children and young women have been rescued. Anti-trafficking policies are now established in nations that did not have them before, and many have dedicated their lives to the cause.

Compassion was the motivator and the conduit for such activation. I have seen entire crowds moved with deep compassion when we have shared just one testimony of a child being rescued. Many have wept at the altars, offering their lives, gifts, prayers, voices, and finances to serve the afflicted. Compassion moved them as His compassion moved me years ago. It is so beautiful to give God such a gift. He sowed compassion and now He is reaping through His people who carry His heart.

Michal Ann Goll is one of my heroes of the faith. She is in glory now, but she both knew and responded to the compassion of God while living on earth and led many to step into acts of compassion.

I am currently serving Michal Ann's vision for Women on the Frontlines, and one of the mandates we carry is the mobilization of women to serve the poor, the afflicted, and the needy. Michal Ann set the bar high for us, and she has left a rich legacy behind. Many are living out the trumpet call she heralded and the example she set. I am one of those. This book is filled with perspective, teaching, testimony, and "heartbeat"—God's heartbeat.

Oh, that we would be compassionate as He is compassionate. Digest the message in this book and you will connect with the power of His compassion that can transform victims into victors—through you—for His glory.

—Patricia King
Founder of Patricia King Ministries and XP Ministries
Apostolic leader serving Women on the Frontlines
www.patriciaking.com
www.womenonthefrontlines.com

INTRODUCTION

—✝—

My personal journey leading to the school of compassion started long ago. It began on the day I was born, when God touched my life with His amazing love and grace.

As my mother was giving birth to me, my body was turned around in the breech position. The labor and delivery process had begun during the early morning hours, so the doctor was not immediately available, though he had been called and was hopefully on the way. The contractions increased in frequency and the transition came, but still no doctor. I began to emerge from the birth canal feet first, but my head had not yet appeared. As a result, from the lack of oxygen, my body began to turn blue. The nurse, who had been there the whole time and had witnessed the entire labor process and the beginning of my delivery, was now faced with a life-or-death decision. She knew the law, which stated that a doctor had to deliver the baby, but she also knew that if she did not do something, I would die from suffocation.

The moment of truth had arrived. Should she follow the requirements of the law, or should she act in compassion and save my life? It did not take her long to make this choice, for she put her hand inside the birth canal, found my mouth, put her fingers in my mouth, and pulled me out.

So, I knew the Lord's lovingkindness from the moment of my birth. I was born on February 14—Valentine's Day—and each birthday I celebrate is like receiving a special valentine from my heavenly Father, a personal affirmation which says, "I love you!" Yes, He is full of loving compassion.

Like Christian in *Pilgrim's Progress,* God is taking me on a journey. When I found myself in the valley of intimidation, He introduced me to a "hall of heroes" like the ones described by the prophet Nehemiah and the writer of the book of Hebrews (see Neh. 7 and Heb. 11).

First, as He introduced me to many heroines of courage, I was drawn to the life of Joan of Arc. She taught me that the darkness of the age we live in does not really matter, because God's light is eternal and He will open every door for us if we truly love Him and desire for His will to be done. As a result, my heart became a flame of passion that filled me with the courage I needed to sever the chains of intimidation that had held me captive for so long; my appetite for more of God became truly insatiable.

Next, I began to devour books about other great women of faith and courage: Vibia Perpetua, Sojourner Truth, Harriet Tubman, Aimee Semple McPherson, Lydia Christensen Prince, Bertha Smith, Corrie ten Boom, and Jackie Pullinger. I wrote about these great women in my book, *A Call to Courage*, and they laid the foundation of my own hall of heroes.

As I built upon that foundation and continued walking through the hallway, the fierier my heart became, and I fell more deeply in love with my heavenly Father, who began helping me build the second level of my hall of heroes. The Lord gave me fresh insights and showed me how He had always been with me, even during the most trying times of my life. I know that He will always be with me.

Through the writings of Madame Jeanne Guyon, I received further spiritual enlightenment and new understandings of God and His ways. Her profound wisdom helped me firmly establish Jesus as the center of my life; when this happened, everything in my life began to fall into place and I discovered a wonderfully deep peace in Him. This brought great healing and strength to my soul.

As I continued on, I studied the lives of Teresa of Avila, Susanna Wesley, Fanny Crosby, Basilea Schlink, Gwen Shaw, and Elizabeth Alves. Oh, the riches I gained from these special women. Like Susanna Wesley, I determined that my prayer closet could be as simple as my apron. I basked in the anointing that rested upon the famous blind hymn-writer Fanny Crosby, whose inspiring and stirring hymns ushered in a vital spiritual awakening in her time and continue to minister personally to people everywhere. These new friends were brought together in my second book in the Women on the Frontlines series, titled *A Call to the Secret Place.* This book releases a sweet fragrance of God.

I am convinced that if we have truly experienced the transformation that always occurs when we abide in His presence, it will cause us to turn outward to bring this powerful transformation to the world. After all, this is the power of the love of God that we have known and experienced. His heart is always reaching out to anyone who will receive Him. If I have truly been set free from fear and intimidation and have been filled with a courageous spirit, and if I have truly found my resting place in the heart of God, I must stir myself to action and move my heart to act on behalf of others.

Therefore, I next looked into the lives of other women who knew this same compelling call and who followed through. These trailblazers are Catherine Booth, Nancy Ward, Florence Nightingale, Gladys Aylward, Mother Teresa, Amy Carmichael, Katharine Drexel, Phoebe Palmer, Hannah More, Elizabeth Fry, and Heidi Baker. These ladies have challenged the prevailing systems and have met the circumstances of life and even governments with gutsy determination, overcoming anything that resisted God's love and power.

I love these women. I want their don't-tell-me-I-can't determination, and I hope you do too. Let's continue our journey with them, and let's bring with us many men and women who desire to love the Lord with all their hearts and to love their neighbors as themselves.

Now I have a few questions for you. What is your heart telling you? Do you want to break open whole regions of the earth for the Lord's heart? Do you want to make a difference in someone's life? Do you want to overcome the limitations that have bound you up and paralyzed you? Then come along with me. Join me on this exciting journey.

As Heidi Baker would say, let's build a whole of company of "laid-down lovers" for Jesus' sake. The Father is waiting for us to fill His house. He is waiting and longing for you and me to take action.

—Michal Ann Goll
Franklin, Tennessee
August 2006

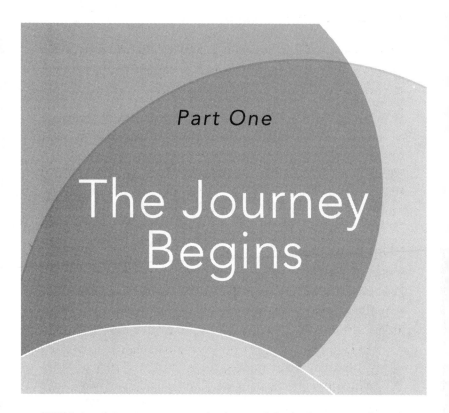

Part One

The Journey Begins

This book is a journey into the heart of God. The journey begins with a look at the source of all compassionate action—God's compassionate heart. You will discover that our compassion is a reflection of the All-Compassionate One. John writes, "The one who does not love has not become acquainted with God [does not and never did know Him], for God is love. [He is the originator of love, and it is an enduring attribute of His nature.] (1 John 4:8). Our love, replicated in our actions toward others, is a reflection of the depth of our relationship with God.

Yes, God is love, and the essence of His being is manifested in His acts toward us. His conduct toward people reveals His compassion for people. Those who bear His nature will also reflect His character in their actions in the human city. He longs for us to become love and compassion in the midst of a world starving for just a little love. In order to do so, however, we must get to know Him intimately and personally, as Jesus did. We must be connected to the Source and allow His love to flow through us. As that love begins to freely flow to us from our Father, it will eventually flow through us to others in loving words and compassionate acts.

In this first section you will learn what compassion is, how God's compassion works, and the power of tears. Jesus frequently wept when He saw the needs of the people and was moved with compassion to do something about them. He sowed in tears and reaped in joy, and you can do the same, for His power and anointing rest upon you.

We must unite our hearts to go forth in compassion to the world. We realize, though, that we still have a lot to learn about converting desire into deed. In many ways our journey has just begun.

Each step of the way, we have learned to look to Jesus, who truly is the personification of compassion. The lives of those who have gone before us will also serve as a source of great inspiration. They will encourage us to reshape our world as they reshaped their world by the love of God.

Our prayer for you is this:

> …that the God of our Lord Jesus Christ, the Father of glory, may grant you a spirit of wisdom and of revelation [that gives you a deep and personal and intimate insight] into the true knowledge of Him [for we know the Father through the Son]. And [I pray] that the eyes of your heart [the very center and core of your being] may be enlightened [flooded with light by the Holy Spirit], so that you will know and cherish the hope [the divine guarantee, the confident expectation] to which He has called you, the riches of His glorious inheritance in the saints (God's people), and [so that you will begin to know] what the immeasurable and unlimited and surpassing greatness of His [active, spiritual] power is in us who believe. These are in accordance with the working of His mighty strength (Eph. 1:17–19).

So, let the journey begin!

Chapter 1

GOD'S HEART OF COMPASSION

(Michal Ann Goll)

On a trip to Thailand, I found myself sitting in a Mexican restaurant in Bangkok. The young ladies who worked as servers were wearing cowboy hats, cowboy boots, and other western wear. I thought it was funny to see such outfits in Bangkok, never mind in a "Mexican" restaurant.

I had been in Thailand for a couple of weeks and had eaten a variety of dishes, some of which caused me to wonder about their ingredients, and I was gaining a little skill in eating with chopsticks. This Mexican restaurant represented my first opportunity to taste more familiar foods and flavors.

My friends and I were having a delightful conversation—a nice respite from our hectic schedule of prayer meetings, travel, sleeping in different hotels, and many, many meetings. As I looked around the room and through the front window, I noticed a young man standing outside. He was holding a sign, and he had several little toys dangling on fine strings all around him.

From the booth where we were sitting, I could read his sign; he was deaf and had created these little toys, which were crickets, out of bits of bamboo. He was selling them for a modest price of twenty baht (approximately fifty cents) apiece so he could buy food.

Though he was a simple and needy young man, he didn't look like he was begging. He stood upright, showed no emotion, and was not really trying to sell us anything. He did not have the typical pleading eyes of a beggar, and he did not gesture for our attention.

I was impressed by how he stood with an air of quiet self-respect and seeming uprightness of heart. We did not exchange a word between us, but our hearts touched each other that day as we peered into each other's souls. I believe I gave him something that day—something far more than the twenty baht it cost me to buy a cricket. I gave him my promise to do all I could with my life, to make a difference in his life and in the lives of others like him.

At the same time, he gave me something, something I desperately needed. He gave me the privilege of touching his life, of making a difference. I caught a glimpse into the heart of God. This young man showed me that you don't have to be somebody who is important or famous; you just have to be available. You have to be willing to engage in the journey and walk the path that Jesus walks every day. This is what the journey of learning God's ways is all about.

Whenever I looked at the little cricket I bought from this young man, I remembered this treasured experience and renewed my commitment to the Lord Jesus Christ. Thus, I continued on the journey that had been set before me.

Do you want more of Jesus? Is your heart engaged with the things that move His heart? Do you want more of the Father's love deposited in your heart?

How can we understand this amazing love that He so

deeply desires for us to experience? His love is beyond our mental abilities to comprehend. Many of us have tainted understandings of what a father is like. Our understanding of fatherhood is shaped by our childhood experiences with our earthly fathers. So, we have to ask ourselves, "What do I really know about God and His heart? What do I really know about His mercy and compassion?" To know His mercy and compassion, we must open our hearts to Him. We must go to the one place where He exposes the tenderness of His heart—into His written Word, the Bible.

Act Justly and Love Mercy

In the book, *The Justice God Is Seeking,* author and our friend David Ruis writes, "Steeped in humility, we are called to act justly and to love mercy. Don't miss this! Justice is an action, to be done in and through the power of Christian community, but mercy is to be loved. It is not an action; it is a passion."[1]

True compassion and mercy stem from a passion for the Father's heart. Do you love mercy? When we learn to truly love mercy and compassion, out of our passion for God's heart, we will be motivated to act justly.

Justice and righteousness form the foundation of the Father's throne. The psalmist writes, "Righteousness and justice are the foundation of Your throne; lovingkindness and truth go before You" (Ps. 89:14).

Go to God's throne of grace as we begin, and ask Him for a grace of impartation and a spirit of revelation to come upon you. Ask God to enlighten your mind and to fill your heart with His fire. Open your heart to the Holy Spirit and let Him speak to you, guide you, teach you, and move you. Let the river of God, which is always full, flow forth in all its energy and power.

The writer of the book of Hebrews says, "Let us then approach God's throne of grace with confidence, so that we may receive mercy and find grace to help us in our time of need" (Heb. 4:16, NIV).

Consider the Weak and the Poor

Did you ever consider the fact that happiness comes from walking in compassion? This is what David meant when he wrote, "Happy are those who consider the poor; the Lord delivers them in the day of trouble" (Ps. 41:1, NRSV). What a glorious promise this is.

The psalmist then goes on to list some of the other benefits to be derived from considering the weak and the poor (see Ps. 41:1–4):

> The Lord will protect us.
> The Lord will keep us alive.
> We shall be called "blessed in the land."
> We will not be given over to our enemies.
> The Lord will sustain us.
> The Lord will refresh us.
> The Lord will strengthen us.
> The Lord will turn, change, and transform us.

These are just some of the things that happen when we are filled with compassion and reach out in love to others. Doesn't this make you want to really be in tune with God's heart as you begin your journey?

God's Heart of Compassion

God's compassions never fail. In fact, they are renewed every day (see Lamentations 3:22). He wants us to keep our hearts open to Him each day as well.

We must be careful to guard against any bitterness or hardness of heart that may try to creep into our lives. God actually commands us to never let our hearts and minds grow hard or cold:

> If there is a poor man among you, one of your fellow Israelites, in any of your cities in the land that the Lord your God is giving you, you shall not be heartless, nor close-fisted with your poor brother; but you shall freely open your hand to him, and shall generously lend to him whatever he needs. Beware that there is no wicked thought in your heart, saying, "The seventh year, the year of release (remission, pardon), is approaching," and your eye is hostile (unsympathetic) toward your poor brother, and you give him nothing [since he would not have to repay you]; for he may cry out to the Lord against you, and it will become a sin for you. You shall freely and generously give to him, and your heart shall not be resentful when you give to him, because for this [generous] thing the Lord your God will bless you in all your work and in all your undertakings. (Deut. 15:7–10)

What does God want from us? Open hands and open hearts and a willingness to help those in need. He wants us to give freely and cheerfully. This is mercy in action, the love of God reaching out to the oppressed.

This passage refers to the seventh year—the year of Jubilee—when all the lands would lie fallow and the slaves would be set free. He warns the people against looking to the seventh year as the time when their needs would be met instead of getting involved in the here-and-now. In fact, God calls such a consideration "a base thought," something that actually leads to sin.

Notice how God tells us to open our hands wide to the needy and the poor in "your land." What is your land? Everyone will have a different answer, depending on the work of God in their hearts. But this we know, "our land" is local; it's home. We are to start at home, but not to stop there. We must enlarge our hearts and do all we can to reach the peoples of every nation, tribe, and tongue.

True Justice

True justice involves both kindness and compassion. Zechariah writes, "Thus has the Lord of hosts said, 'Dispense true justice and practice kindness and compassion, to each other; and do not oppress or exploit the widow or the fatherless, the stranger or the poor; and do not devise or even imagine evil in your hearts against one another" (Zech. 7:9–10).

Do you see the relationship between justice and compassion that is portrayed here? In order to understand God's plumb line of justice, we have to know what He values. In fact, the Lord showed me something I had never seen before (story just below), and when He did so, He said to me, "Mercy without justice enables thievery!"

This helped me to understand that our concept of mercy and compassion is limited. In fact, many times it is askew. All too often people think that mercy, simply stated, is *pity*. Though pity is certainly an element of mercy, true mercy and compassion involve so much more.

God always acts from both justice and mercy, and you really can't have one without the other. Sometimes the most merciful thing is to say no to someone who is seeking something from you, particularly if you are looking at the person's stated need through the eyes of both justice and mercy.

The boundaries of the field of mercy and compassion must be firmly established and clearly delineated. We don't ever want anything to encroach on territory that belongs to the Lord and is set apart for the poor and needy.

While I was in Mozambique one time, I observed some children who were beggars from a nearby village. There are many needy children there, since disease, war, poverty, and drought have ravaged the land and torn families apart. Many children have no parents because they have died from AIDS or other causes. Many children beg, but some have learned how to "work the system."

In a church service one Sunday morning, a few boys entered the tent (sanctuary) for the sole purpose of seeing what they could get from people. They could spot the new visitors. These unsuspecting people gathered these young boys in their arms, not engaging in spiritual discernment. They just wanted to bless these children.

The problem was that this particular group of boys was looking for things they could steal and sell later. They worked their plan, getting into camera cases and people's bags. While one would occupy a person, one or two others would look for what they could steal. As I watched this situation unfolding, I began to understand that some of them were actually operating out of demonic activity in order to steal from people.

This is where discernment comes into play. We need to be sure that the one in front of us has a genuine need before we attempt to respond to that need. Did the boys have a legitimate need? Yes. And as food was always served in that place, they could have had the opportunity to fill their stomachs. But what was the condition of their hearts? They also had the opportunity to come to know Jesus; but they were on a different mission. They were in church to steal. The attention that was given to those boys denied other dear children who really could have used that love, those hugs, that attention. The children who were really needy, with open loving hearts to the Lord, suffered because of the others' thievery.

Here's another story. One man who was with us had brought several deflated soccer balls to Mozambique because he knew the children there rarely get to see one. One boy came up to him and began begging for money. The man gave him a soccer ball instead. A short time later, the boy returned. He had ruined the ball, and he began to demand money in exchange for it. Even if he couldn't use the ball, or didn't want it, he had no concept of giving it away to someone else. His mind was consumed with the love of money. This was true thievery. The boy had destroyed the ball so nobody else could enjoy it.

We need to understand what mercy and compassion are according to God's standards, not according to the standards of humans. From His point of view, compassion must always involve justice.

True Judicial Government

God wants governments to rule with justice, righteousness, and compassion, but we all know that this is not always the case. The psalmist writes:

> God has taken his place in the divine council; in the midst of the gods he holds judgment: "How long will you judge unjustly and show partiality to the wicked? Give justice to the weak and the orphan; maintain the right of the lowly and the destitute. Rescue the

weak and the needy; deliver them from the hand of the wicked." (Ps. 82:1–4, NRSV)

Here we see God's heart concerning true judicial government. Such a government should not show partiality, and it should always do justice to the poor, the fatherless, the afflicted, and the needy. In fact, it should even deliver the poor and needy and rescue them from the wicked.

As followers of Jesus, we should do everything within our power to make sure that this is the kind of government we have. We should vote for godly candidates, and we should vote the wicked out of office. God might even call us to run for public office ourselves so that His justice, righteousness, and mercy can take hold where we live. It is time to stand up in the seats of government and let our lights shine.

God's Heart Concerning Honor

The following Scripture shook me to the core of my being as its truth penetrated my spirit: "Whoever oppresses the poor shows contempt for their Maker, but whoever is kind to the needy honors God" (Prov. 14:31, NIV). I don't know how this could be any clearer.

Do you want to honor God? If your answer is yes, you must operate in kindness and mercy to the needy. To do otherwise brings contempt, mockery, and insult to God.

God's Heart Concerning Lending

Proverbs 19:17 (NIV) says, "Whoever is kind to the poor lends to the Lord, and he will reward them for what they have done." This reminds me of what Jesus said: "Truly I tell you, whatever you did for one of the least of these brothers and sisters of mine, you did for me" (Matt. 25:40, NIV).

What you give to the poor, you give to God, and He promises to repay you.

God's Heart Concerning Righteousness

God equates righteousness with care for the rights of the poor: "The righteous man cares for the rights of the poor, but the wicked man has no interest in such knowledge" (Prov. 29:7). Look at the contrast that is painted for us here. Whereas the righteous person knows and cares for the rights of the poor, the wicked person is completely uninterested in anything like that.

I would like to think of myself as a righteous person, but there have been many times when I've had to repent of my lack of mercy and my unwillingness to tune my heart to God's heart. My desire is to be like the woman who is described in Proverbs 31: "She opens and extends her hand to the poor, and she reaches out her filled hands to the needy" (Prov. 31:20). This verse shows a righteous woman in action.

God's Chosen Fast

Once I had a dream in which I saw twenty or thirty people standing all around me. It seemed that they had been witnesses of my life. One particular man who was standing over me had a spirit of prophecy resting on him. He reminded me of an old-fashioned water pump, the kind where you prime the pump first and then start moving the handle up and down. I sensed that, as this man moved from side to side, the water of God's Word was building up inside him.

In this dream I was very sick. My body was crumpled over an old stone wall, and I was crying, "Will someone get me a doctor? I'm very, very sick!"

Everybody stared at me, and the man I mentioned said, "Don't you know you've been called to prayer and fasting?"

I said, "I need help. Will someone please get me a doctor?"

Again, he said, "Don't you know you've been called to prayer and fasting?"

I whimpered, "Please! Somebody help me! Please! I need help!"

The man stood in front of me and repeated, "Don't you know you've been called to prayer and fasting?" Then he added, "Don't you know that if you would enter into prayer and fasting, you would extend the orphan's bread from three to five days?"

This question hit me hard. I began to see that what I needed was not a doctor after all. What I really needed was to obey the Lord by entering into prayer and fasting.

I have always been really terrible at fasting. God's chosen fast, however, goes beyond the issue of food and flesh; it goes deep into your heart. God's chosen fast becomes a lifestyle that we are called to embrace. What is His chosen fast? The Bible tells us, "[Rather] is this not the fast which I choose, to undo the bonds of wickedness, to tear to pieces the ropes of the yoke, to let the oppressed go free and break apart every [enslaving] yoke?" (Isa. 58:6). Now that's a powerful fast.

Have you entered a fast that shares your own bread with the hungry? Have you brought the homeless into your home, covered the naked, and provided for the needs of your family and all those around you? (See Isa. 58:7.) This is God's chosen fast, and it is truly an exciting fast in which to get engaged, for this is always its result:

> Then your light will break out like the dawn, and your healing (restoration, new life) will quickly spring forth; your righteousness will go before you [leading you to peace and prosperity], the glory of the Lord will be your rear guard. (Isa. 58:8)

The Compassion of Jesus

David Ruis writes, "As followers of Jesus, we cannot ignore what moved Him to send out the first of His disciples, what moves Him still to send us out today: compassion. Biblical compassion is a uniquely Christian virtue."[2]

Jesus always saw the need first, then He was moved with a compassion so strong that it always led Him to do something in response to the need. Matthew writes, "When he saw the crowds, he had compassion for them, because they were harassed and helpless, like sheep without a shepherd" (Matt. 9:36, NRSV).

He then went on to tell His disciples to pray that God would send laborers into His harvest. We need to engage in the same kind of prayer today, for so many people are confused like sheep without a shepherd. God is looking for people who will go out into the fields that are now white unto harvest (see Matt. 9:37–38).

The Greek word for compassion (pity and sympathy) that is used here is *splanchnizomai,* and it means to be moved deep within. It involves a sense of yearning in behalf of others.

If you have compassion, you will be moved to take action, as Jesus always did and still does. God wants you to know His compassion, receive His compassion, live His compassion, and share His compassion with others.[3] All the Scriptures within this chapter open God's heart to you. He is your loving heavenly Father, and He wants you to share in His compassion. I agree with David Ruis, who writes:

> To touch Christ is to touch compassion. Far beyond a guilt-trip, a tweaked conscience or a pale sense of pity, compassion reaches into the very guts and

demands action. It compels prayers that will move heaven, intercessions that cry out for workers to be thrust into this weighted-down harvest. It motivates one to move—to go and set it right—to administer justice through the power of the Kingdom.[4]

Compassion will move so deeply within your being that many times you will find yourself moved to the point of tears and agony. God places great value in your tears, and as we turn to the next chapter, you will discover this is a deep well that moves heaven on behalf of others.

Heavenly Father, I come to You right now in the name of Jesus. I ask You to light the fire of passion in my life and let it become the kind of compassion that doesn't just look at the need, but looks to You. Help me to become so passionate for loving You and knowing Your heart that I will move in compassion to all those in need. I ask that You will bring about a corporate shift of thinking and acting in the entire body of Christ, that Your people would become passionate about compassion by being passionate for You. I ask that You would take the Scriptures in this chapter and drop their truths deep within my heart. Let Your Word continue to flow within the depths of my spirit so I will be able to receive all the spiritual nutrients you have for me. Drop Your plumb line of justice through all of my thoughts and feelings, all of my traditions and training, and let me learn to do justly and to love mercy and to walk humbly with You. In Jesus' name, amen.

＋

Chapter 2

THE COMPASSIONATE POWER OF TEARS

(James W. Goll)

Jesus frequently used the word "behold" when He was teaching His disciples the truths about His kingdom. In so doing He was telling them to open their spiritual eyes and see the truth He was conveying.

When Jesus saw the throngs of people who were suffering as a result of their sins, He was moved with compassion for them. Often, He even wept over them. The shortest verse in the Bible says, "Jesus wept" (John 11:35). What was He weeping over? First, He saw the need, which was the death of Lazarus.

Then He heard the cry of Martha's heart: "Master, if You had been here, my brother would not have died" (John 11:21). At this point Martha expressed her faith in the Master's ability to heal. She said, "Even now I know that whatever You ask of God, God will give to You" (John 11:22).

Next, Jesus heard the piercing cries of Mary, the sister of Martha and Lazarus, and "When Jesus saw her sobbing, and the Jews who had come with her also sobbing, He was deeply moved in spirit...and was troubled" (John 11:33).

Because He saw and listened actively to the heart cries of Martha, Mary, and the assembled Jews, and because He was tuned in to the resonance of the heart of Father God Himself, Jesus was moved with compassion. In turn, He ministered effectively to the urgent need at hand—Lazarus came forth from the tomb, demonstrating resurrection power.

Tears preceded this power encounter. Perhaps compassion and power are inevitably linked. Yes, our tears have the power to cleanse, to enable us to see, and to thrust us into action in behalf of those in need.

Whenever we hear God speaking to our hearts, we need to obey His inner promptings. As good parents raising their children frequently say, "Just listen and obey!" Obedience brings action to our feelings. Obedience demonstrates commitment to our inner convictions and moves us beyond ourselves.

Bowels of Mercy

Jesus was frequently moved with pity, sympathy, and compassion for the people He saw around Him. He really saw them, and He saw their needs. This means He was fully aware, perceptive, understanding, and responsive to them.

Often, the Lord saw people as being bewildered, like sheep without a shepherd, and this deeply troubled Him, as we see in the Gospel of Mark: "When Jesus landed and saw a large crowd, he had compassion on them, because they were like sheep without a shepherd. So he began teaching them many things" (Mark 6:34, NIV).

It has been accurately said that when a need is presented to us, we really have three options:

- To be inactive—to do nothing. Like the proverbial ostrich, we can choose to stick our heads in the sand and hope the problem will go away.
- To be reactive—this is an emotional response, usually in the form of anger, to a troubling situation.
- To be proactive—this involves taking positive steps to rectify the problem.

Jesus, when He was moved with compassion, was always proactive. In the case just cited in the Scripture, we see that He responded to the disorientation He saw in the people by commanding kingdom order in their lives.

As we go forth in compassion, we need to do more than express only sympathy or pity. As Jesus did, we need to do something concrete to help others. Perhaps the best help we can give others is to teach them how to overcome through faith, prayer, and spiritual understanding. We need to exemplify kingdom authority right out in the open, as Jesus did, for all to see. The kind of compassion Jesus walked in was not weak and passive; it was tender yet tough, sensitive yet confrontational.

Jesus' heart was (and is yet to this day) filled with compassion. Jesus modeled compassionate living in personal ways for both individuals and for the masses. He practiced what Paul preached:

> Therefore, as God's chosen people, holy and dearly loved, clothe yourselves with compassion, kindness, humility, gentleness and patience. Bear with each other and forgive one another if any of you has a grievance against someone. Forgive as the Lord forgave you. (Col. 3:12–13, NIV)

Can there be any more vivid portrayal of compassion than this? This is a verbal picture of what God expects from each of us. It is the "bowels of mercy" that the King James Version of the Bible tells us to "put on."

The "bowels" are found deep within us, and the fountain of tears that flows when our hearts are filled with mercy comes from deep within our spirits, where the Holy Spirit, who groans in compassion with "unspeakable yearnings and groanings too deep for utterance" resides (see Rom. 8:26).

So, listen and obey. Let compassion flow forth from your innermost being—your bowels of mercy. Remember, it is out of practicing His presence that compassion is born. The love of God works inward (within you), but, as it works inward, it always begins to move outward.

Seven Doors

One evening, my friend Marcus Young and I were waiting on the Lord together. I received a remarkable spiritual vision of seven consecutive doors, which I told about in full in my book *The Lost Art of Practicing His Presence.* Let me give you an overview of that God encounter:

I saw in the spirit a succession of seven doorways, and over each one there was a word written. The word "Forgiveness" was engraved over the first door. As I crossed over the threshold of that first door, I was able to see what was written over the second door: "Cleansed by the Blood."

This helped me to understand that sometimes, though we know we are forgiven, we might not have fully realized or experienced the reality of total cleansing through the blood of Jesus Christ. As I passed through the second doorway, I experienced the cleansing power of the blood in a new and total way. I knew I was truly cleansed by His blood.

I went on through the third and fourth doorways; they dealt with areas of holiness and sanctification through the power of the Holy Spirit. Then I came to the fifth doorway and noticed that its title was "Grace." As I walked through that portal, a new revelation of the grace of God came upon me.

I learned much as I continued in this interactive vision. I discovered that grace empowers the believer with the anointing, and I also learned that all of God's giftings are received by grace. These are what I call "gracelets," little drops of grace. I learned that the degree of anointing one has comes from passing through God's doorway to grace. It is then that the oil of the Holy Spirit begins to fall on us.

The word "Mercy" was prominently displayed over the sixth doorway. Whereas grace had dealt with God's action toward me, I now learned that mercy had to do with our actions toward others.

This was a very long passageway, but at its end I could make out what was written over the seventh door: "Union With Christ." I wanted so desperately to get to the seventh door, but I knew I couldn't do so until I had completely passed through the sixth corridor—the realm of mercy. This realization filled my heart with anguish.

All I could do was cry, "Lord, teach me your mercy," for I knew then that the only way I would ever be able to enjoy complete union with Christ would be by walking in mercy and compassion at all times.

Sympathetic Consciousness

Compassion involves a sympathetic consciousness toward others. More simply stated, it is being stricken in your heart with a sensitive spiritual awareness of others' hurts, positions, distresses, and dilemmas. More than that, it involves having a divine motivation to do something about their situation. The following verse gives us insight into the heart of compassion at work:

> Brothers, if anyone is caught in any sin, you who are spiritual [that is, you who are responsive to the guidance of the Spirit] are to restore such a person in a spirit of gentleness... (Gal. 6:1)

The Lord Jesus has a heart of compassion toward each one of us, as we see in Hebrews 4:15:

> For we do not have a high priest who is unable to empathize with our weaknesses, but we have one who has been tempted in every way, just as we are— yet he did not sin. (Heb. 4:15, NIV)

Jesus knows about our struggles. He shares our feelings and bears our burdens with us. He truly understands what we are going through. It is this knowledge that enables us to "approach God's throne of grace with confidence, so that we may receive mercy and find grace to help us in our time of need" (Heb. 4:16, NIV).

We really do have a High Priest who sympathizes with us and gives us His mercy. He is our compassionate Lord and Savior. The psalmist puts it this way: "The Lord is good to all; he has compassion on all he has made" (Ps. 145:9, NIV).

His Compassions Fail Not

Jeremiah wrote, "Because of the Lord's great love we are not consumed, for his compassions never fail. They are new every morning; great is your faithfulness" (Lam. 3:22–23, NIV).

These verses give us a clear understanding of the heart of our Father and the way He deals with His children. The late

John Wimber shared a revealing testimony in his outstanding book, *Power Healing*[1:]

One day, as he was praying, he was discussing an observation with the Lord about how many people, including himself, are sometimes afraid to pray for the sick. As he contemplated this idea, he began to understand that this may well be due to the fact that many do not understand God's nature and how He works. Then the Lord spoke to John and told him that most people are hesitant and even fearful about praying for another's healing because they misunderstand His compassion and mercy. The Lord told him that many know *about* Him but they do not really *know* Him.

This word from the Lord empowered John to go forth in faith and compassion and, as a result, God used him as a vehicle through which His healing mercies flowed, but his joy was tempered somewhat when he received a rather disturbing vision from the Lord. As he was driving, he saw what looked like a cloud bank in the sky. He pulled his car to the side of the road. Then he realized it wasn't a cloud that he was seeing after all; it was a honeycomb filled with honey, and it was dripping on the people below.

Some people were eagerly gulping down the honey, loving its sweet taste and offering it to others. Other people, however, were irritated by the sticky honey that was being poured all over them, trying to wipe it off and complaining about "the mess."

The Lord explained to John that the honey was His mercy, which to some is a blessing and to others is a hindrance. He told John that there was plenty for everyone and that we shouldn't beg Him for healing, because the problem isn't on His end; it is with the people.

Like Jesus, we need to weep over the people who are

wandering like sheep without a shepherd. Often they just do not understand who God is, what He has already accomplished on Calvary, and what He wants to do for them.

Try Tears

General William Booth, who founded the Salvation Army with his wife, Catherine, received several letters from people who were lamenting over the seeming lack of progress in their ministries. In their letters they expressed little hope about saving the lost. They said that things were too hard and that it appeared as if nothing was happening.

Booth's response to them was very simple. He tore off a piece of a brown paper, wrote a note on it, and sent it to the seekers. Poignantly, it stated, "Try tears."[2]

We need to let our hearts be broken with the things that break the heart of God. One pastor put it this way: "My church will never grow while my eyes are dry."

What a splendid way this is of expressing the strong burden that comes when our hearts are broken before God. Basilea Schlinck wrote, "The first characteristic of the kingdom of heaven is the overflowing joy that comes from contrition and repentance, tears of contrition soften even the hardest hearts."[3]

Tears of contrition come from our brokenness before God. They express our utter abhorrence of our sinfulness and our complete dependence upon the Lord for everything. David Brainerd, a well-known missionary to American Indian tribes, recorded the following entry in his diary on October 18, 1780:

> My soul was exceedingly melted and bitterly mourned over my exceeding sinfulness and vileness. I never before felt so pungent and deep a sense of the odious

nature of sin as at this time. My soul was then carried forth and loved to God and had a lively sense of
God's love to me."[4]

This was an experience that Brainerd had as he was praying while standing in the snow on a bitter winter day. He was
smitten with a great revelation of His utter dependence upon
and absolute need for God, and he saw his own sinfulness
in a new light. But God didn't leave him there; He gave him
a greater revelation of Himself and His great love for him.

The Prayer of Tears

Compassionate praying, as David Brainerd's experience
shows, is prophetic praying. It deals with the deep-seated
desires of the spirit, a craving for that which does not pres-
ently exist. It is deep calling unto deep (see Ps. 42:7). This
involves profound yearning, crying, groaning, longing, and
earnestness that come from deep within you. It is the beginning of the prayer of tears.

The prayer of tears is a form of compassion in action. It
works in an intercessory and prophetic fashion, touching the
lives of those we pray for. As we engage in compassionate
praying, God puts His heart within us. We actually receive an
impartation of something that is not of ourselves, and we are
moved with tenderness, sensitivity, and mercy. This allows us
to actually feel the pain of another person at least for a while.
We could say that this is the "gift of pain," a gift in the sense
that it is a supernatural impartation of compassion, the ability to suffer with those who suffer (see 1 Cor. 12:26).

My dear brother Mahesh Chavda was praying for me
one time, and the Holy Spirit began to speak to me. He
said, "I am going to give you the gift of pain." Now, this
was a message that I wasn't too sure about, as you can well

imagine. The Holy Spirit went on, "I'm going to give you the gift of pain, and you will feel my feelings temporarily in your being, your body."

The word "temporarily" helped to ease my anxiety over this message a little bit. It was then that an entirely new spiritual understanding came to me. I began to realize that it is possible to feel the sufferings of others for a while when we are interceding for them. I think what happens is that God actually puts His heart, which breaks with compassion for others, within us for a while so that we will be truly able to bear their burdens before His throne.

As you wait before the Lord and give Him your heart, He will touch you with a portion of His burden and give you His heart to enable you to carry others at least for a while before His throne. When this happens, it's as if you become a little donkey—a beast of burden—for Him. In this way God puts His burden upon you.

The Holy Spirit concluded what He was saying to me with this sentence: "I'm going to give you the gift of pain, and you will feel the fellowship of My sufferings, and you will feel the pains of others, and then, as you release this and bring it back to Me, the pain will lift."

Then I realized how glorious it is to be smitten with the things that break God's heart. Indeed, it's one of the greatest privileges we could ever have. To think that God in all of His glory and grandeur would share His heart with us and give us His pain is mind-boggling. It truly is an honor to be a donkey for Him.

The Fellowship of His Sufferings

Paul writes that his determined purpose is, "...that I may know Him and the power of His resurrection, and the fellowship of His sufferings, being conformed to His death" (Phil. 3:10, NKJV). We can join the fellowship of Christ's sufferings. This enables us to rejoice with those who rejoice and to weep with those who weep (see Rom. 12:15). The God of compassion and all comfort is always there to help us (see 2 Cor. 1:3–4). David writes, "My sacrifice, O God, is a broken spirit; a broken and contrite heart you, God, will not despise" (Ps. 51:17, NIV).

The great evangelist and writer Charles Finney knew and practiced the truth of this verse. He had a weeping heart. He often went into the woods north of his village to pray, and he confessed that he did this so that others would not see him. He writes, "An overwhelming sense of my wickedness in being ashamed to have a human being see me on my knees before God took such a powerful possession of me that I cried at the top of my voice, and I exclaimed that I would not leave, and I proclaimed that I would not leave this place, that if all the men on earth, and all the devils in hell surrounded me. I prayed until my mind became so full that before I was aware of it I was on my feet and tripping up the ascent towards the road."

Though he had gone into the woods at dawn, when he reached town it was already noon. He had been so deep in prayer that time had lost all meaning to him. He later went to dinner but discovered that he had no appetite for food, so he went to his office to play hymns on his bass viola, but he found that he couldn't sing without weeping.

He shares what happened as that night progressed: "All my feelings seemed to rise and to flow out, the utterance of my heart was, I want to pour out my whole soul to God. The rising of my soul was so great, I went…back to the front office to pray, I wept like a child, and made such confession as I could with my choked utterance. It seemed to be as though I bathed His feet with my tears."[5]

This weeping servant sowed precious seed into the lives of two and a half million people who came to know the Lord Jesus Christ as their personal Savior. Research tells us that at least 75 percent of these converts remained true to Christ till their deaths.

This is what we need today—men and women of God who learn the power of tears, the compassion of Christ, the importance of prayer, and the fire of the Holy Ghost.

Do What Matters

A few years ago, in one of those times of transition that God loves and we tend to disdain, I was fervently seeking the Lord. Like a shepherd guiding His sheep, Jesus my Great Shepherd responded to my passionate prayer and gave me a dream of wisdom and guidance. In this enlightening dream, I was soaring through the heavens like an American kestrel, a bird that is noted for its ability to hover in the air against even strong winds. Sometimes the kestrel appears to be standing still in midair. So, here I was, flying like a bird through the air when suddenly everything stopped. Next, I received a tremendous revelation.

I saw a beautiful garden next to a great stone wall and an attractive stucco-covered house. It was as if I was looking at this scene through a camera's zoom lens. I saw a spectacular array of multicolored flowers and then saw a woman in a red dress; she was bent over, working in the garden.

Somehow I knew this woman was my Aunt Mae, a wonderful, godly woman who had inspired my life at a very early age. I remembered the details of her scarlet red dress. She looked up at me and slowly said, "Do...what...matters."

That's all I heard in the dream, and then the revelation was over.

This was a pictorial representation of my mother's oldest sister, and she was giving me a very important message as she worked in her garden as she had always loved to do. Aunt Mae gave her life to serve others. She remained single all through her life, and fully presented herself to God so He could use her as He desired. This wonderful lady impacted my life in so many important ways in my youth, and I still miss her today, though she has been with the Lord for many years now.

In the dream her voice said, "Do what matters," and I knew immediately what the Lord was referring to. What's important in this life? Paul says, "…The only thing that counts is faith expressing itself through love" (Gal. 5:6, NIV).

As you get the heart of God, which is love, you can't help but do what matters.

Brought Back by the Tears of a Friend

When I was in Prague some time ago, I learned that one of the main pastors, Evald Ruffy of a Moravian church, would not be able to be with us because he had suffered a heart attack while ministering in Sweden, and he was in a coma.

His best friend, Peter, called for Christians throughout the Czech Republic to pray for Pastor Ruffy. As he traveled to Sweden to be with the pastor, Peter felt as if he was actually taking the prayers of the saints with him. He said that he could definitely feel the power of their prayers as he walked into the hospital.

An eruption of the Holy Spirit took place within Peter in the entranceway of the hospital, and he was stirred with compassion deep within. Meanwhile, Pastor Evald had already spent three days with God in heaven, where he discovered many spiritual mysteries. He was able to look down upon the earth from his heavenly vantage point, and he saw dark clouds all over Central and Eastern Europe. While beholding this scene, he noticed white lights going up and down through the black clouds. He asked his Guide, the Holy Spirit, "What is this?"

"Well, the dark clouds are the territorial spirits of darkness that are over Central Europe."

The pastor raised another question: "What are those white lights?"

"Oh, those are My angels, and they are breaking up the powers of darkness over Central Europe."

"How does this happen?" the pastor asked.

"Oh, this happens in answer to the prayers of the saints."

Pastor Evald was greatly enjoying this special experience that God was giving to him unbeknownst to Peter, who was now standing by his friend's bed feeling somewhat helpless. In his weakness, Peter began to cry, weeping profusely over his friend. When his tears streamed down his face and fell onto his friend's face and body, something amazing happened.

Those tears that splashed upon Evald's face caused him to realize that his work on earth was not over. He still had more to do as a husband, father, and pastor. His eyes opened, and he was instantly released from the coma that had imprisoned and immobilized him. In fact, he was totally healed. Even his doctors declared that what happened to him was a miracle.

The power of tears had brought healing to a man of God, a modern-day apostle who went on to establish many Spirit-filled evangelical Moravian churches in Eastern Europe.

Intercessory prayer combined with compassionate weeping is a powerful force that truly brings change in our world today. As William Booth declared, "Try tears!"

Do you want to move in compassion? Then receive compassion. Do you want to move in healing? Then receive healing. Do you want to move in deliverance? Then receive deliverance. Whatever you receive by faith through the love of God you will be authorized to give away.

Stop by the gateway of the sixth door as I have, and drink deeply from the brook of mercy. This will enable you to continue to move forward in your walk of being more like Jesus and to empower you to do the works of Christ.

Jesus said, "Freely you have received, freely give" (Matt. 10:8, NKJV).

Heavenly Father, your Word declares that you welcome those who have a broken and a contrite heart. Give me your great grace so that I can walk in unison with Your heart. Help me to humble myself before you, leaning on Jesus. Lord, grant me the gift of tears and a compassionate heart, so that I can see life spring forth where it seems hopeless and lifeless. I desire your heart, Lord, and I cry with streams of tears, as Joel did so long ago, "I rend my heart in hope that You will bring forth newness of life, victory, healing, joy, and compassion to those in need." In Jesus' great name, amen.

Part Two

Lives of Compassion

Part Two is devoted to eleven women who have spent their lives in compassionate service to God and others. These women and many others have pioneered the way so that God's compassion might be expressed in new and creative ways in the lives of countless millions of people around the world.

May your heart be stirred as you read these stories, and may they become sources of inspiration so that you will live a life of compassion in your own world.

Chapter 3

Catherine Booth

THE MOTHER OF THE SALVATION ARMY

(Michal Ann Goll)

A true heroine of faith and compassion, Catherine Booth, paved the way for the liberation and deliverance of women, children, the downtrodden, the forgotten, the lost, and the dying. And from her courageous example we can learn so much.

In Catherine's time very few women ever rose to speak to a church congregation. One day, however, as Catherine was sitting in the Gateshead Bethesda Chapel, she felt a strong urging to rise and speak. As she prepared to do so, she heard an inner voice say, "You will look like a fool and have nothing to say!"

She recognized the voice as being the devil, and she countered with, "That's just the point! I have never yet been willing to be a fool for Christ. Now I will be one!"[1]

I love this lady and the wonderful determination she exhibited in the face of seemingly insurmountable odds, although it is difficult to separate her life and accomplishments from those of her husband, William. William and Catherine exemplify a "Barak and Deborah" kind of anointing. Their ministries blended together and overlapped; the ministry and anointing of one made the other's possible.

"God shall have all there is of William Booth!"

William Booth was born on April 19, 1829, in Nottingham, England. His father, Samuel, was a builder, but the economic conditions were very poor in England at this time, which meant that the homes he built were not selling. He could neither sell nor rent the homes he built, so he eventually lost everything, including the mortgage on his own house.

Though he had great plans for William, including a good gentleman's education, Samuel did not have enough money to make this happen for his son. Therefore, when William was thirteen years old, he was apprenticed to a pawnbroker in a horrible part of Nottingham, where homeless people had to live in the streets.

Less than a year later, Samuel Booth died, so William was faced with the dismal prospects of having to support the family, which included his mother and his sisters. Eventually, his mother was able to find a job running a small shop, and between their two incomes, they managed to keep food on the family table.[2]

As a result of working in such a poor part of the city, William saw firsthand how the poor had to live and how miserable most of them were. He responded to the misery he saw around him with a sense of gloom and despair until one night in 1844, when he was walking home after work.

Suddenly, a sense of spiritual exaltation flooded his entire being. This was very much like John Wesley's Aldersgate Chapel experience, when the founder of the Methodist Church felt his heart "strangely warmed." In William's case he responded by renouncing his sin and turning his heart and life over to the Lord. This was the earnest declaration he made that night: "God shall have all there is of William Booth!"

Soon thereafter, William began to blend his social consciousness with his newfound faith, and a great desire grew within him to see an organization formed that would have the salvation of the world as its supreme ambition and goal. His perspective was a practical one; he wanted to meet the real needs of people. Therefore, he wasn't very much concerned with ecclesiastical creeds, rituals, and forms.

Several preachers, including the American revivalist James Caughey, held evangelistic meetings in Nottingham in 1846, and they became William's mentors. He learned a great deal about God from these men. He also read the sermons and books of John Wesley, George Whitefield, and Charles Finney, particularly Finney's *Lectures on Revivals of Religion.*

William and his friend Will Sansom joined their hearts and hands together by determining to make a difference in the lives of the people of the Meadow Platts neighborhood, another very poor section of the city. Theirs was a roll-up-your-sleeves kind of faith that wasn't afraid to reach out and touch the actual needs of people. The compassion these men had in their hearts for the "down and outers" of society made them unafraid to act on behalf of others.

These two men did more than just hold meetings; they went on to visit and encourage those who made decisions for Christ, and they visited the sick in the community as well.

This was a time when the average life expectancy, due to disease and other factors, was short—only thirty-five to forty years of age. Unfortunately, Will Sansom died soon after the two men began their ministry. It was then when William began conducting open-air meetings for the poor in Red Lion's Square and "down in the bottoms," one of Nottingham's cruelest neighborhoods.

Booth wrote, "I saw terrible sights—ragged, shrieking people, little children foraging for food, dirty women, some clad only in soiled petticoats, more little children—these appeared drunk, with their mothers forcing beer down their throats—whimpering, hungry dogs, men's faces with animal passion written all over them as they watched dancing women in the street."[3]

Later, in a letter he sent to Catherine from London, he wrote,

> I've been told that there are 3 million souls in London, and 100,000 paupers. After what I've seen this week, I know it's true. Many of these people are on the brink of starvation.... Catherine, the people are sick, some of them dying, some are already dead. And the smell...the whole city stinks, I couldn't escape it.... I've found my destiny. It's a human jungle out there. I've been walking in the midst of it.... It's as bad as any tiger-infested jungle in darkest Africa.

Because of his hard work and his passion for the poor, William Booth became known as "Willful Will." He was very much like the American evangelist Dwight L. Moody, who ministered in Chicago later in that same century. Moody said that the world had yet to see what would happen when one man gave his life unreservedly to the Lord, and he said he intended to be that man.

"My God, I am Thine!"

Now let's take a closer look at the life of Catherine Booth, who was born on January 17, 1829, in Ashburn, Derbyshire. Her maiden name was Mumford, and her father was a rather unstable individual who exhibited very erratic behavior. At one time he had been a lay preacher in the Methodist Church, then he became a temperance advocate who preached vigorously against alcohol, but finally he became an alcoholic himself. He was prone to wild swings of uncontrollable emotions, which created an environment of disorder and uncertainty for his daughter as she was growing up.

As the child of an alcoholic, Catherine knew firsthand what happens to families affected by alcoholism. By the time she was twelve, she was able to attend a girls' school and became the secretary of the Juvenile Temperance Society, and she had read the Bible all the way through eight times. Catherine's mentors included Charles Finney and John Wesley, and she read many of the same works that her future husband had read.

When Catherine was fourteen, she developed a spinal curvature; then, four years later, she was diagnosed with incipient tuberculosis. She was home-schooled during much of this time. Because she was isolated from other children her age, she was able to cultivate her relationship with her heavenly Father. She read the Bible and also studied church history and theology. This was when her writing career began, as it was while she was sick in bed that she began writing magazine articles that warned of the dangers of alcohol, and she became a supporter of temperance societies.[4]

When Catherine was sixteen, she had a radical conversion experience in church on a Sunday morning. This happened because she took to heart the words of a hymn written by Charles Wesley: "My God, I am thine, what a comfort divine, what a blessing to know that Jesus is mine." She surrendered her life to the Lord Jesus Christ, and she knew that He took up His residence in her heart.

Catherine and her mother were attending a Wesleyan Methodist Church at this time, but like so many others, including William, they got caught in the division between the Wesleyan Methodists and the Reformers, who had broken from the Methodist Church because they perceived it to be cold and lifeless, too conservative for their tastes. Both William and Catherine were expelled from the Methodist Church because they favored the Reformers.

Their relationship with the Reformers did not last long, however, for the Reformers stressed strong organization and a lot of committee work, which many perceived as detrimental to the more important work of revival.

She became a strong advocate for the unlimited involvement of women in all aspects of worship, teaching, and leadership in the church. In that regard, Catherine Booth was definitely a woman who was ahead of her time.

What God Has Joined Together

In 1852 Catherine met William Booth, a Methodist minister. By this time the Methodist church had lost some of the fervor it had known during the previous century, when the Wesleys—John, Charles, Samuel, and their mother, Susanna—had been instrumental in bringing great change to the church.

William Booth, however, was on fire for God, and he believed that ministers should be involved in "loosing chains of injustice, freeing the captive and oppressed, sharing food and home, clothing the naked, and carrying out family responsibilities." He was a man who was committed to compassionate reform.[5]

Though they loved each other deeply, William and Catherine did have their differences. One of these involved the role of women in the church. These were days in which women were not permitted to minister in the church. Even William Booth regarded them as "the weaker sex," and this aggravated Catherine very much. She could not believe how prejudiced her husband was with regard to women, and she said, "Oh, prejudice, what will it not do, that woman is in any respect, except physical strength and courage, inferior to man, I cannot see cause to believe, and I am sure no one can prove it from the Word of God."

Initially William was strongly opposed to the idea of women preachers, and he based this position on what Paul had written: "Let your women keep silent in the churches, for they are not permitted to speak; but they are to be submissive, as the law also says" (1 Cor. 14:34, NKJV). I believe that this Scripture has been misinterpreted for centuries, not taking into account that Paul was referring to women who had previously been temple prostitutes, or who were newly converted to Christianity, and therefore untaught in appropriate behavior and customs for a Christian context.

However, Catherine believed that God loved women as much as He loved men and that He had endowed women with qualities and gifts that were equal to those He gave to men.

As time went on, William began to rethink his position on this issue, and he said, "I would not encourage a woman to begin preaching, although I would not stop her on any account." His focus was on the salvation of the world, so he said, "I am for the world's salvation; I will quarrel with no means that promises help." Here we see his attitude concerning the role of women beginning to undergo some change.

Catherine said, "What can we do to wake the Church up?

Too often those who have its destinies in the palm of their hands are chiefly chosen from those who are mere encyclopedias of the past rather than from those who are distinguished by their possession of Divine Power. For leadership of the Church something more is required."[6]

This couple, despite their differences, was sold out to God. Catherine once wrote these words to her husband: "The nearer our assimilation to Jesus, the more perfect and heavenly our union." They knew that for their marriage to work, they had to put God first.

William was now beginning to learn things about his wife that he had not known before. He discovered that in conversation she was someone who could hold her own with anyone. She was a very intelligent lady who was conversant about many different things.

For example, she was able to discuss current trends in the churches of England, and she was very much concerned about the controversy swirling between the Revivalists and the anti-revival movement. In addition, Catherine understood the plight of the poor.

Sometimes William would fall victim to fits of gloom and depression. At such times Catherine would stir him up again and give him fresh reasons for battling on. He began to recognize her as his equal and to see that her capacity for work and self-sacrifice was as strong as his. She was both a stimulant and a stabilizer for her husband.

Catherine's compelling and heart-touching writings became well-known throughout England, and she became known simply as "the woman preacher." In the early days of her public ministry, she spoke these strong words about her role: "I dare say many of you have been looking on me as a very devoted woman, but I have been disobeying God. I am convinced that women have the right and duty to speak up; yes, even to preach! I have struggled with this for a long time, but I'll struggle with it no longer."

When William heard his wife preach, he completely changed his mind about women preachers. He did so in spite of the fact that many people judged him for doing so and continued to feel that women preachers were unbiblical.[7] Lord Shaftesbury, a well-known politician and evangelist, actually declared that William Booth was the antichrist due to his attitude toward women preachers. This did not seem to faze William, however, for he commented, "The best men in my army are the women."[8]

Catherine went on to teach Bible studies, visit in the homes of the poor, and reach out to women who were greatly abused and oppressed. She made this observation, "The plight of the women is so pathetic."[9] Here we see the birth of a woman preacher, who became a heroine and mentor to thousands of women, but she was never ordained. Nonetheless, during the first few months of 1861, while the Civil War was raging in America, Catherine began accepting invitations to preach in public.

She and William served in several different communities, including Gateshead, a town of 50,000 that is located just across the River Tyne from Newcastle, on the northeastern coast of England.

When William became sick during the summer of 1860, Catherine had to take over all his duties, for it took him several months to recover. As a result, her remarkable abilities became known to many and her fame as "the woman preacher" grew far and wide.

Trailblazer for Women

In nineteenth-century England, as a result of the Industrial Revolution, poverty, crime, disease, corruption, prostitution, alcoholism, and immorality were rampant. We read about some of these conditions in the socially realistic novels that were written by Charles Dickens.

The Beer Bill of 1830 allowed pubs to be legally open from 4:00 A.M. to 10:00 P.M., and many people would spend their meager wages on beer and ale. Decades of beer drinking brought forth an entire generation of drunkards who lost sight of all moral values. Mothers would even serve beer to their small children, who became alcoholics before they reached puberty.

Working conditions were horrendous for everyone, especially women and children. While working with the poor in London, Catherine Booth learned about "sweated labor," women and children who had to work long hours for very low wages in the worst imaginable conditions.[10] In certain London tenements Catherine found seamstresses, for example, who had to hem and stitch for eleven hours or more each day, and their pay was abysmally low.[11]

Catherine's work among the poor grew into a ministry that seemed as powerful as her husband's preaching, and she continued to preach the gospel despite the many criticisms she and her husband received.

When she became aware of a pamphlet that was written by a Rev. A. A. Reese, which was a diatribe against the ministry of Phoebe Palmer (who ministered in both England and America and who had written *The Way of Holiness* and *Faith and Its Effects*), Catherine responded by writing a booklet of her own titled *Female Teaching: or the Reverend*

A. A. Reese vs. Mrs. Palmer, Being a Reply to a Pamphlet by the Above Named Gentleman on the Sunderland Revival, in which she voiced her support of Phoebe's ministry.

Catherine Booth was a true trailblazer for women, and she was a model of Christian compassion at work in the world.

The Fruit of Their Labors

The Booths' first evangelistic work began on August 11, 1861, in Cornwall County. Originally planned as a seven-week revival, the crusade was extended to an eighteen-month campaign, unparalleled in that part of England at least since the time of John Wesley.

At least seven thousand Cornishmen found peace with God during this year and a half. It was even reported that fishermen sailed ten miles across dark and choppy waters to hear the young couple preach. Similarly, it was not unusual for villagers to walk several miles to attend the meetings. As a result, many shop owners experienced a great decline in sales, because people's hearts were turning away from material things.

There was a great hunger for God in the hearts of the people. This included Catherine's father, who returned to the Lord. The Booths' outreach was not limited to church people, and they discovered that people who frequented the pubs were "more likely to go through a tent flap than through an oaken church door to find God."

William Booth recognized the fact that clergymen weren't reaching the people who had the greatest needs, and he wondered how he would be able to unite his ministry with that of the local church. Many of the new converts, when they went to churches, were greatly disappointed by the stale traditionalism they found there. He wanted his converts to be able to find a "church home."

Therefore, the Booths began to look for ways to connect evangelism to the local church.

Bringing the Poor and the Wealthy Together

Another cry in the hearts of William and Catherine Booth was to find a way to bring the poor and wealthy together. Therefore, William boldly took the poor into the wealthiest churches of Nottingham. His approach was not well-received by the established church.

As a result of the friction, the Booths left the Reformers and joined a group called the Methodist New Connection, which had a strong Wesleyan foundation, supported revivalism, and encouraged lay people to get involved in the decision-making. This organization's magazine provided Catherine a great opportunity to continue her writing ministry.

Then in the spring of 1857, at the annual conference of the Methodist New Connection, William was removed from his position as a full-time evangelist because some of the leaders of the organization were no longer comfortable with his methods. They had made him take a regular preaching circuit in an effort to force him to focus on pastoral responsibilities rather than evangelism. The particular circuit to which they assigned William was obscure and unsuccessful. The leaders must have felt that this was the perfect place to "keep him out of trouble." William endured this assignment but did not really like it, and in the meantime Catherine's ministry continued to flourish.

The following year William was ordained as a minister, and his next pastoral assignment was in Gateshead. This was when real release began to happen in the Booths' ministry and their evangelistic outreach began to surge. At this point the young couple began to experiment with publicity, and they distributed handbills door to door throughout every neighborhood. They also conducted street meetings, which consisted of hymn-singing, exhortations, and invitations to attend church services.

In an effort to meet the needs of people where they were, the Booths began to take the popular melodies and tunes of their day and adapt them for use as gospel songs. They made their ministry relevant to the needs of the people.

Before their meetings would begin, the Booths would set aside an entire day of prayer, and this had a great impact on the services, paving the way for the Spirit of God to find entrance into the prepared hearts and lives of the people who attended. William and Catherine loved the people, and the people responded to their love, which reflected the Father's heart to them.

The Salvation Army Is Born

On August 7, 1878, William declared his vision for the Salvation Army. He said, "To postpone action any further will be an act of disobedience to what we both sense is the divine will of God."

Catherine was in full support of this declaration. She said, "William, don't hold back because of me. I can trust in God and go out with Him, and I can live on bread and water. Go out and do your duty. God will provide if we will only go straight on in the path of duty."

At this point they broke with the Methodist New Connection and began their own independent evangelistic ministry. The distinguishing features of this ministry were authority, obedience, the adapted employment of everyone's abilities, the training and discipline of all workers, and the combined action of all.

They adapted army jargon in their work. William believed very much in the chain of command, and he became a general, whose job was to oversee the ministry. They trained the people who worked with them and taught them how to endure and rise above the mocking of the crowds in the street, which sometimes occurred. The idea of uniforms began to emerge at this point as well, and the bonnets for the women were designed in such a way as to protect them from rotten eggs and garbage that were sometimes thrown at them.

The Booths expected their workers to go into the most distressful situations and love the most needy, the most hurting, and sometimes even the most hateful. They also believed in the importance of combining their forces like a mighty army as they reached out to those in need.

At this stage in their lives, William and Catherine Booth were both only thirty-two years old. They had five children and very little money. They settled in Leeds, a town in the English midlands, and began to conduct separate campaigns so as to increase their effectiveness.

Hundreds of adults and children responded to the invitation to find Christ under Catherine's preaching ministry. Her preaching, along with the success William was experiencing in his ministry to the poor, came to the notice of *The Revival*, England's premier evangelistic journal. As a result, William was invited to preach in White Chapel in early 1865. White Chapel was a poor section in the notorious East End of London. He asked Catherine to preach there as well.

Soon thereafter, Catherine became aware of the Midnight Movement for Fallen Women, an agency that combined evangelism with social redemption. Her experience with this organization opened her eyes to the need for social concern to become a part of their ministry. Catherine began to see a need to champion the cause of women, and she advocated for them to be placed in positions of responsibility and usefulness within the church. Through her preaching in the West End, she touched the hearts and lives of people who could help provide financial support for the struggling work William was doing in the East End.

When speaking publicly, Catherine never minced her words. She spoke with boldness and righteous indignation as she confronted the evils of her day. In so doing she made the comfortable less comfortable, and she even went so far as to accuse affluent Christians by saying that they were responsible for the sweatshops and the filthy working conditions in which women and children found themselves.

Once she made this statement: "It will be a happy day for England when Christian ladies transfer their sympathies from poodles and terriers to destitute and starving children."

The Booths then created the East London Christian Revival Society, which became known as the East London Christian Mission or, more commonly, the Christian Mission. The name was later changed to the Salvation Army. Catherine became the primary promoter of this ministry, while William continued to work among the poor in the East End. What a team they were, with Catherine doing the preaching and raising the funds, and William in the slums ministering to the needs of the poor.

Early on, their children learned what ministry was all about. Their oldest child, William Bramwell Booth, was dedicated to God when he was born. Catherine said, "I held him up to God as soon as I had strength to do so, and I remember specially desiring that he should be an advocate of holiness."

Ballington, their second son, began to see himself as a preacher when he was eleven. He even preached to his sisters' dolls. One of his "new converts" was a pillow in a chair. Looking at this pillow, he was heard commanding, "Give up the drink, brother!"

The younger children were Kate, Herbert, Emma, and Marion, who was an invalid, and then along came Evangeline Corey, who eventually became the first woman general of the Salvation Army, and Lucy. The Booths had a total of eight children, and each became active in the work of the Salvation Army. Their children said that Catherine not only patched their clothing, but she even made them proud of the patches.

Bramwell recalled that his father once took him into a pub in the East End of London where he saw the men's alcohol-inflamed faces and observed drunken, disheveled women nursing their babies. Although he was nauseated by the pungent aroma of gin, tobacco, and sweat, his father turned to him and said, "These are our people; these are the people I want you to live for and bring to Christ."

Catherine Booth organized Food-for-the-Million shops, where the poor could afford inexpensively priced hot soup and three-course dinners. On special occasions such as Christmas, she would sometimes cook more than three hundred dinners that were distributed to the poor.

By 1882 there were almost 17,000 people worshiping under the auspices of the Salvation Army, far more than the attendance in mainline churches. This caused the Archbishop of York, the Rev. Dr. William Thornton, to comment that the Salvation Army was reaching people that the Church of England had failed to reach.

Since those early days and more than a century later, the Salvation Army remains a vital force in the world. As a result of the army's ministry, new laws protecting women and children were enacted in England. The impact of the Salvation Army was reached around the world, and its ministries have included prison work, youth work, rescue homes for women, ministry to alcoholics and drug addicts, rescue missions, salvage operations, disaster relief, and men's hostels.

The Salvation Army has earned the respect of the White House, the United States Supreme Court, embassies around the world, the U.S. Congress, and governments in many nations.

Catherine Booth was the mother of the Salvation Army—a true "mother in Israel." She knew that *compassion acts*. She knew that it is born out of passion for the Father's heart. She wrote, "Don't let controversy hurt your soul. Live near to God by prayer. Just fall down at his feet and open your very soul before him, and throw yourself right into his arms."

Father God, thank You for the wonderful example of Catherine Booth. Help us to be like her, people who fall at your feet and open our souls before you. I throw myself into Your arms, dear Father, and ask You to light the fires of passion in my heart, that I would be aflame with Your love and go forth in compassion to those who need to know how much You love them. Let me become a true agent of change in the world, as I act in mercy to others. Give me Your wisdom, Lord, so I can see things from Your point of view. Help me not to lean upon my own insight, but to trust You for all things. As I acknowledge You, I know You will direct my path. In Jesus' name, amen.

—†—

Chapter 4

Nancy Ward

Nan-ye-hi (Nancy Ward), *Ghighau* (Beloved Woman)
of the Ani-Yunwiya (Principal People)

BELOVED WOMAN
OF THE CHEROKEE

(Ada Winn, with Dr. J. Mark Rodgers)

A fresh wind is blowing within the body of Christ. Across denominational, racial, and political lines the Spirit of God is exposing the roots of ritual-based, Christian religion. This exposure is showing many of us ways in which our religious expressions have supplanted an authentic relationship with the Father.

Whether or not we like to admit it, the cultures that most dramatically shaped our nation as we know it were those of the Greeks and Romans. Even in this modern era, their societies continue to influence government structures, health care delivery systems, educational institutions, and, perhaps most importantly, religious structures in America. The third-century Roman Church is responsible for when we worship, where we worship, how we worship, and with whom we worship. It is said that Christian faith conquered Rome and then Rome conquered Christianity. It is out of a conquering mind-set that most people view American history. Could it be that God views the United States differently?

Over the millennia, European societies exploited environmental conditions for the purpose of gaining greater wealth and opulence. Wealth represented power, and power, in turn, control. During this same time period, Native American societies lived in cooperation with their environment; in contrast to exploitation, they practiced stewardship. When Europeans arrived on the continent of North America, they found a pristine environment that showed little impact from thousands of years of human habitation. It is out of those thousands of years of stewardship that we examine the life of one Native American we know as Nancy Ward.[1]

Her native name was Nan-ye-hi. In the custom of many Europeans, white people anglicized her name to Nancy. Out of respect for her, I will use her native name for the remainder of this chapter.

Nan-ye-hi was born sometime around 1737 in Chota, the capital of the Cherokee Nation. She was described as a strikingly beautiful woman with a tall, erect figure, prominent nose, piercing black eyes, and silken black hair. Because her skin was tinted like a reddish-pink rose, she was given the nickname Tsistuna-gis-ka, or Wild Rose. As she grew older, Nan-ye-hi matured with a stately but kind disposition, carrying herself in a queenly and majestic way.

Cherokee societies were matrilineal. Warriors received their status in the tribe from their mother's lineage, not from their father's. In this matrilineal society, women were stewards of the land, not the men. The women enjoyed more matrimonial rights than men; upon marriage, the men became members of their wife's clan, with their homes along with the contents belonging to the women. Children belonged to the mother's clan. It was into matrilineal lines of the tribal leadership that Nan-ye-hi was born.

Her mother was said to have been Tame Doe. Tame Doe was a niece of Old Hop, who was a principal chief. One of Tame Doe's brothers was Attakullakulla, a celebrated peace chief. Historians rated him as one of the most influential leaders among the southern tribes. He was named Little Carpenter by the whites because of his diplomatic skills, which included fitting parts of peace treaties together into a workable diplomatic document.

Nan-ye-hi married early by today's standards. She married Kingfisher when she was only sixteen years of age. Kingfisher was a leader within the tribe, and his leadership was tested during one of the fiercest battles recorded in Cherokee history, the battle of Taliwa in 1755. Led by their great war chief, Oconostota, the Cherokee were determined to drive the Creeks out of their land. Creek opponents reportedly outnumbered a five-hundred-man Cherokee war party. In support of her husband during this battle, Nan-ye-hi was chewing the musket balls for his rifle, in hopes that they would become more jagged and lethal.

There were war whoops and screams, the sound of musket fire, and the yelling of commands over the din of the battle. In the midst of the fight, Kingfisher was struck down with a mortal wound. I imagine that husband and wife glanced at each other for one brief moment realizing the tragedy that had befallen them. When this sixteen-year-old bride witnessed the flicker of life leave her husband, Nan-ye-hi distinguished herself from other women. Even though it was common for a woman to support her warrior husband, it was very uncharacteristic to join in the battle and continue the fight. Her unwavering bravery that day rallied the Cherokee warriors and routed the Creeks from northern Georgia.

After the appropriate time of mourning, the tribe celebrated Nan-ye-hi's efforts in this nationally significant battle by bestowing upon her the honor of Ghighau or "Beloved Woman." Nan-ye-hi was in her teens when vaulted into her high position—an honor ordinarily bestowed on older women.

Ghighau was more than a term of endearment; it enabled Nan-ye-hi to participate in negotiations for treaties, to commute death sentences passed upon by tribal leadership, and to prepare portions of ceremonial offerings given to the men of the tribe. The Beloved Woman title was a lifetime distinction. During state council meetings in the townhouse, Ghighau sat with the peace chief and war chief in the holy area near the ceremonial fire. As head of the women's council, she would represent the view of women in the tribe. The female council did not hesitate to vote to oppose the decisions made by the ruling headsmen, particularly if they felt that the welfare of the tribe was at stake. It was during the lifetime of Nan-ye-hi that tribal leadership passed all but two of the land cession treaties with the Cherokee.

During the 1700s, European settlers began in earnest to encroach upon Cherokee lands. The surge of newly arriving immigrants increased annually. These newcomers pressed westward as settlements grew crowded in the east. They saw vast stretches of wilderness seemingly uninhabited except for scattered tribal villages, and all native people were viewed as inhabitants with no recorded claim or title to the land. As rising unrest was apparent (the colonies were preparing for war against British rule), westward expansion continued.

Trade between the native people and Europeans was more like exploitation than marketplace equality. English traders' demand of animal skins increased yearly. Up until 1750, an average of 54,000 deerskins per year were shipped from Charles Town (today known as Charleston, South Carolina). By 1759, it is said that over 1.5 million deerskins were shipped annually through the Charles Town port. This "big kill," as it is called, almost exhausted the deer population in the South.

The fledgling independence movement found its way across the Appalachian Mountains into what is now eastern Tennessee. Having to face either the tyranny of British rule or hostile tribes, some chose to face the Cherokee. Despite stern warnings from the Crown of England for all white settlers to leave native land west of the Appalachian Mountains, settlements at Watauga and Nolichucky were created.

The Cherokees' first reaction was not war. The Cherokee tribal council negotiated a ten-year lease agreement with the Wataugans. In exchange for this land lease, they were to receive the equivalent of a $1,000 per year in trade goods. Their desire was to live peacefully alongside the white settlers while they remained stewards of the land. The Wataugans also agreed to no further encroachment on native lands. There was a peaceful coexistence during the early years of the lease, but this peace was short-lived when the settlers annexed more land without providing trade goods as promised.

After many violated treaties by the settlers, a battle erupted with the Wataugan and Nolichucky settlements during the summer of 1776. Nan-ye-hi sent messages to Fort Watauga and the surrounding communities warning of an attack. Some might question her motives in warning the settlers; however, her desire was to live peacefully with the white population. The Cherokee, led by Dragging Canoe, Nan-ye-hi's cousin, were defeated by the settlers due to her warning before the attack, and the attack on Fort Watauga was repelled.

During this battle, Chief Old Abram captured two prisoners who were taken back to Cherokee villages. One of the captives was a Mrs. William Bean. Tied to a pole with leather thongs, she had dry tree branches laid around her feet and lit on fire. When Nan-ye-hi learned of the planned execution, she kicked the burning branches away, stomped out the remaining small flames, and cut the throngs, freeing Mrs. Bean. She then addressed the angered warriors and spoke with harsh words, "It revolts my soul that Cherokee warriors would stoop so low as to torture this woman. No woman shall be tortured or burned at the stake while I am Honored Woman."

This incident shows Nan-ye-hi exercising her official position as Ghighau. Nan-ye-hi led Mrs. Bean to her home in Chota, the town of sanctuary, and asked Mrs. Bean to teach her and the members of her family how to process cow's milk to make butter and cheese. She was hoping to encourage interest in her people for raising their own meat and farm crops, since dependence solely on dwindling wildlife, resources of the forest, and expensive supplies would spell certain failure for her people. Nan-ye-hi also learned the art of weaving cloth, or "homespun," from Mrs. Bean. When it was safe to do so, Nan-ye-hi sent Mrs. Bean back to her home. Nan-ye-hi's son, Fivekiller, and her brother, Longfellow, escorted Mrs. Bean to protect her during the journey.

It was sometime during this time when Nan-ye-hi met a trader named Bryant Ward. Some believe that she and her friends protected the life of this trader during a time of hostility. Bryant Ward and Nan-ye-hi were married shortly thereafter. As a woman in a matrilineal society, she had rights to take a husband as she pleased, even when her choice was outside of her race. What is more interesting is that she took his last name in direct conflict with her cultural upbringing. You may recall that the men took their wife's heritage after marriage. Nan-ye-hi was sending yet another message that it was possible to make changes in order to preserve a way of life.

Throughout Nan-ye-hi's life, her tribe was approached many times about additional acquisitions of land. Very few of the treaties signed with the native peoples of America were kept by either the British or American governments. Hostilities continued to flare as native warriors retaliated for white encroachments, and white settlers exacted their revenge on native populations for what they felt were atrocities. Nan-ye-hi found herself continuously in a place of attempting to mediate between warring factions.

One time when the Cherokee were going to war against the white settlers, Nan-ye-hi again found herself forewarning frontier settlers of an imminent attack by Dragging Canoe. She saw that every time the Cherokee were on the warpath, her nation suffered tragically. She had witnessed indiscriminant killing on both sides. Perhaps she hoped that by sending her warning, much bloodshed could be avoided.

Nan-ye-hi never acted alone in any of these warnings to frontier settlers. Her tribal leadership had met and voted to continue peacefully, but the warring chiefs would not listen to those who were in leadership. In sending warning of attack, Nan-ye-hi was representing what she thought was the true nature of official tribal leadership.

A new treaty was demanded by the Cherokee in order to

prevent future battles with the new American colonies. Nan-ye-hi rose from the negotiations and eloquently addressed both parties present: "You know that women are always looked upon as nothing, but we are your mothers. You are our sons. Our cry is all for peace. Let it continue. This peace must last forever. Let your women's sons be ours, our sons be yours, let your women hear our words." The sincerity and appeal of her words reached the hearts of her listeners.

Colonel William Christian was chosen to answer Nan-ye-hi's comments. He said, "Mothers, we have listened well to your talk. It is humane. No man can hear it without being moved by it. Such words and thoughts show the world that human nature is the same everywhere. Our women shall hear your words and we know how they will feel and think of them. We are all descendants of the same woman. We will not quarrel with you because you are our mothers. We will not meddle with your people if they will be still and quiet at home and let us live in peace." This is one of the very few treaties, if not the only one, that did not ask for land.

Her speech placed Nan-ye-hi in the ranks of great women of America. The time of her talk was July 1781. Nan-ye-hi had witnessed the burning and pillage of her tribe. She had every right to be bitter in seeing everything she loved destroyed; however, she chose a different path—the path of peace. It took fortitude and character for any woman warrior not to strike back.

By 1784, Nan-ye-hi Ward's home in the beloved town of Chota could no longer remain a prominent place in Cherokee history. It was burned and pillaged first by the British and later by American colonists. Legend has it that prior to Nan-ye-hi moving from Chota, she opened her home to orphaned native children (mostly outcast and abandoned children of white traders and native women), perhaps the only real sanctuary these youngsters ever enjoyed. A Lieutenant Francis Marion wrote with eloquent terms what he saw take place:

> We proceeded by Colonel Grant's orders to burn the Indian cabins....I saw everywhere around the footsteps of little Indian children where they had lately played under the shade of their rustling corn. When we are gone, thought I, they will return and, peeping through the weeds with tearful eyes, will mark the ghastly ruin where they had so often played. 'Who did this?' they will ask their mothers, and the reply will be, 'The white people did it, the Christians did it.' Thus, for cursed mammon's sake, the followers of Christ have sowed the selfish tares of hate...

Nan-ye-hi remained an advocate for her country and nation for several years. She continued to speak of the necessity of her people to devote more attention to farming and raising stock as a means of survival. One of Nan-ye-hi's last treaties with the Cherokee, Article 14 of the Holston River Treaty, guaranteed their ability and assistance in husbandry and agriculture as they would continue to prosper in their land.

Nan-ye-hi Ward addressed her nation for the last time on May 2, 1817:

> The Cherokee ladies now being present at the meetings of the chiefs and warriors in council have thought it their duty as mothers to address their beloved chiefs and warriors now assembled.
>
> Our beloved children and head men of the Cherokee Nation, we address you warriors in council. We have raised all of you on the land which we now have, which God gave us to inhabit and raise provisions. We know that our country has once been

extensive but by repeated sales has become circumscribed to a small tract, and never have thought it our duty to interfere in the disposition of it until now. If a father or mother was to sell all their lands which they had to depend, on which their children had to raise their living on which would be indeed bad, and to be removed to another country, we do not wish to go to any unknown country which we have understood some of our children wish to go over the Mississippi. But this act of our children would be like destroying your mothers. Your mothers, your sisters ask and beg of you not to part with any more of our lands we say ours. You are descendants and take pity on our request, but keep it for our growing children, for it was the good will of our creator to place us here and you know our father, the great president will not allow his white children to take our country away. Only keep your hands off of paper talks, for it is our own country. For if it was not, they would not ask you to put your hands to paper for it would be impossible to remove us all. For as soon as one child is raised, we have others in our arms, for such is our situation and will. Consider our circumstance.

Therefore children, don't part with any more of our lands but continue on it and enlarge your farms and cultivate and raise corn and cotton and we your mothers and sisters will make clothing for you which our father, the president, has recommended to us all. We don't charge anybody for selling any lands, but we have heard such intentions of our children. But your talks become true at last and it was our desire to forewarn you all not to part with our lands.

Nancy Ward to her children: Warriors take pity

and listen to talks of your sisters. Although I am very old yet cannot but pity the situation in which you will hear of their minds, I have great many grandchildren, and I wish them to do well on our land.

This address was taken to the council meeting by Nan-ye-hi's son, Fivekiller, and accompanied by her distinctive walking cane, which represented her official vote and authority in her absence.

Nan-ye-hi made one final attempt to stay on her land prior to her death. One stipulation of the 1817–1819 treaty had a reservation clause: "Each head of a Cherokee family residing on lands herein or hereafter ceded to the United States who elects to become a citizen of the United States shall receive a reservation of six hundred and forty (640) acres to include his or her improvements for life, with reversion in fee simple to children, subject to widow's dower." Nan-ye-hi's Reservation number 767 was registered with United States government, but the state of Tennessee flatly refused to recognize these individual reservation grants.

Nan-ye-hi died in the Amovey district near the Ocoee River at the home of her brother, Longfellow. Her white husband had left her for other relationships, although they continued to be friends. Ward's white family reportedly received her with great respect when she visited on occasion. She lived a long and fruitful life, and was called by some Princess and Prophetess.

Nan-ye-hi and those she represented planted many seeds in her nation that would not come of age until after her death. By the time of the Indian Removal Act of 1838, the Cherokee Nation had a form of government similar to that of the colonies. They had a supreme court, a tribe-elected leadership, a written language, a newspaper, and had adapted many of the ways of the colonists. It was against the Cherokee constitution for anyone to hold official office within the nation who did not have a belief in God. The unofficial Cherokee national anthem became "Amazing Grace."

I had the privilege of visiting Nan-ye-hi's homesite near Benton, Tennessee. Her gravesite is now a Tennessee Historic Site. There is a tangible, honorable stillness there. This chapter about the life of Nan-ye-hi is not simply a historic visitation for me as an individual. My family was in Fort Watauga during the time period of Dragging Canoe's attacks. Nan-ye-hi's two warnings to these settlements may well have saved my family's life—and ultimately, my own. Could it be that neither my children nor I would enjoy this life without her compassion for the early settlers of Tennessee?

As I walked her land, my heart was grateful for the compassionate acts of this wonderful lady I have never met. Who else walks this country today who does not know they are alive because of Nan-ye-hi? I felt as if people were watching from past generations.

Nan-ye-hi might have never worshiped in a church. Yet Scripture challenges us that authentic relationship is evident by visible fruit of the outward life we lead.

Less than 5 percent of native people profess a true relationship with Christ; they see Christianity as white man's religion. Many more than this, though, offer a yes to the response of being a Christian. This yes is tempered with generations of those who have been given the choice of being seen as "civilized" Christians or being killed. Most tribal people cannot find cultural identity within traditional Roman Christendom. Roman Christendom defines all facets of the Christian faith currently in America, from Roman Catholics to the independent charismatic church.

Fire is important to the Cherokee. Women were keepers of the fire in their homes. Each year the women ceremoniously extinguished all flames within the tribe. One of the roles of the Ghighau was to reintroduce new fire. In countless ceremonies Nan-ye-hi would have helped in rekindling the fire within her tribe. It was said that if the principal people kept the fire burning, the Creator God would reveal truth. An eternal flame now burns at Red Clay, Tennessee, which was the last capital of a united tribe called the Cherokee prior to the Trail of Tears.

Jesus, you are part of the tribe of Judah. You are a man of color, not a white man. You wore traditional clothing, and power was associated with it. You celebrated the many feasts of your Father. Your tribe's calendar is kept in cycles of the moon. Your Bible is a tribal book. You celebrated your ancestors. Your nation was led by tribal elders. Throughout your tribe's history, animals played important roles. Your Bible celebrates the created order.

You celebrated the land of your inheritance. You took nothing from it you did not need. Your nation fought fiercely all those who attempted to take your land from you. You upheld all your tribal laws. Your Father held your nation accountable to past generations who did not keep their covenants. You are a person who always keeps your word. You allowed false counsel to be spoken of you, without taking revenge, for the sake of your tribe.

You died a tortured death at the hands of a conquering nation to save your people. All who come to you for their salvation are not saved apart from being engrafted into your tribe.

—

Chapter 5

Florence Nightingale

THE LADY WITH THE LAMP

(Michal Ann Goll)

Florence Nightingale was known as "the lady with the lamp," a nickname that was given to her by British soldiers who were wounded during the Crimean War in the mid-1850s.[1] They called her this because they always saw her carrying her lamp as she walked the halls of the hospital each night. Now this name has become a symbol of all that Florence stood for—care for the sick, concern for soldiers' welfare, and freedom for women to choose what kind of work they want to do.

This founder of the modern nursing profession was not the romantic, gentle, retiring Victorian woman that some people might imagine. She was a bright, tough, driven professional who became a brilliant organizer and one of the most influential women of the nineteenth century.

Florence was named for the city where she was born—Florence, Italy. Her date of birth was May 12, 1820, and her wealthy parents were on a two-year-long honeymoon trip through Italy when she was born.

She spent most of her childhood on the family estates in England with her mother, Fanny; her sister, Parthenope; and her father, William. Both of the girls were taught at home by their father, who was a graduate of Cambridge University. He tutored them in languages, history, and philosophy, while their mother taught them the social graces.

Florence excelled in her studies, and she was a very lively and attractive young lady. Her parents probably expected her to be a refined woman of class and distinction who would eventually marry a rich young man—but the Lord had different plans for her.

When she was seventeen years old, God spoke to her heart at Embley, the family's winter home. She wrote, "On February 7, 1837, God spoke to me and called me into His service."[2]

She felt strongly that He had given her a special mission in life. She suspected that this mission would involve helping others, something that Florence had always enjoyed doing. Often, she would care for the babies of her parents' visitors, and she would help care for caretakers on her father's estates when they got sick. Later in life, she wrote: "O God, Thou puttest into my heart this great desire to devote myself to the sick and sorrowful. I offer it to thee. Give me my work to do."[3]

She became a single-minded young lady and even turned down offers of marriage from various suitors, including one young man for whom she felt great love. Instead of attending parties to which she was invited, she would spend her time studying health and social reforms for the poor. Her mother had a hard time with this, because such things were simply not proper for wealthy young women of her day.

Florence had deep compassion in her heart for women

and children who had to work in deplorable conditions. She was concerned about the poor in her own land and the economic and political situation in Ireland. It is clear that she cared about every social issue of her day.

She made regular visits to the sick in nearby villages and began to study the nursing systems of hospitals. Nursing wasn't really a formal profession at this time, and many of the people who helped in hospitals were prostitutes, former servicemen, and drunks. Therefore, nursing was not considered a noble profession.[4] In light of this, you can imagine how horrified Florence's parents were when she told them that she wanted to be a nurse. They tried to discourage her from going out to help the sick.

The Call Gets Clearer

In the spring of 1844, Florence became convinced that her calling was to nurse the sick, but she had her own health struggles to deal with first. In 1850, her family sent her to Egypt in order to recuperate, and while she was there she kept a diary, which details her dialogue with God about His calling in her life. Some of her journal entries follow:

> March 7, 1850—"God called me this morning and asked me would I do good for Him, for Him alone without the reputation?"

> March 9, 1850—"During half an hour I had by myself in my cabin settled the question with God."

> April 1, 1850—"Not able to go out, but wish God to have it all His own way. I like Him to do exactly as He likes without even telling me the reason."

> May 12, 1850—"Today I am 30, the age [when] Christ began his mission, now no more childish things, no

more love, no more marriage, now, Lord, let me think only of Thy will, what Thou wouldst me to do, oh, Lord, thy will, thy will."

June 10, 1850—"The Lord spoke to me. He said, 'Give five minutes every hour to the thought of Me, couldst thou but love Me as Lizzy loves her husband, how happy wouldst thou be.' But Lizzy does not give five minutes every hour for the thought of her husband, she thinks of him every minute, spontaneously."[5]

God had given Florence this time to draw closer to Him. She heard Him speaking to her, and she was ready to go forth in full-flowered compassion to help those in need.

At St. Bartholomew's Hospital in London, Florence met Elizabeth Blackwell, the first woman who ever qualified to be a physician in America. Dr. Blackwell had to overcome all kinds of opposition to enter the medical profession, and Florence was greatly impressed by her. Blackwell encouraged Florence to keep on pursuing her goals.

Eventually her father reluctantly agreed for her to train as a nurse, so, when Florence was thirty-one years old, she went to Kaiserwerth, Germany, in order to be trained at the Lutheran Institute of Protestant Deaconesses, which was running a hospital there. Her training period lasted two years.[6]

Obedience to the Call

Upon her graduation from the nurses' training, Florence went to work at a hospital for invalid women that was located on Harley Street in London. She was appointed as the resident lady superintendent there. While in this position, the new nurse began to think of innovations that might be employed to help the sick. For example, she developed a system of dumbwaiters, which enabled food to be delivered directly to each floor. Previously, nurses had to carry trays of food up several exhausting flights of stairs.

Florence also invented and installed a system of call bells that would enable patients to ring for nursing help from their beds. The bell would sound in the corridor and the valve that was attached to it remained open, enabling the nurses to see who had called for help. She also had the water heater for the hospital installed on the top floor so that hot water would run down, making it much more accessible to the nurses.[7]

The Crimean War

In March 1853, Russia invaded Turkey. Britain and France were concerned about the rise of the Russian Empire, so they responded to the invasion by declaring war on Russia in March 1854. This was the beginning of the Crimean War.

Many soldiers had to endure great hardships as they fought in this bloody war. The death rate was very high due to wounds, typhus, cholera, malaria, and dysentery. Within a few weeks after the conflict began, eight thousand men were in medical facilities.

The *London Times* exposed the poor medical care that was being given to the British soldiers. This caused a public outcry for greater medical care, and Florence Nightingale responded to this need by offering her services. There was still considerable prejudice against women being involved in medicine in any capacity, so the British government officials rejected her offer at first. As time went on, however, they changed their minds because the need was so great.

Florence was given permission to take a group of thirty-eight nurses to the military hospitals in Turkey. When she arrived at the Barak Hospital in the suburbs of Constantinople on November 4, 1854, Florence found the conditions appalling. The doctors who were there seemed to resent having female nurses, so they said, "Don't do anything until we tell you."

Florence reported that many of the men did not have blankets or nutritious food. They were unwashed and still in their uniforms, which were "stiff with dirt and gore." Many were infested with lice, and conditions there permitted only thirty men to be bathed each day—with the same sponge. Florence calculated what this meant: each patient would get bathed only once every eighty days, and it was a very poor bath indeed. She remarked, "Perhaps it was a blessing not to be bathed!"[8]

As the number of wounded increased, the doctors decided that they needed the new nurses after all, though they still objected to many of Florence's views with regard to reforming the system.

Blankets were rotting in warehouses instead of providing warmth for the men because no one had issued the proper paperwork to allow them to be distributed to the patients. The lavatories in the hospitals had no running water, and the latrines were open tubs that had to be emptied by hand, but they were never emptied because no one knew which department was responsible for them.

This resulted in a foul stench wafting throughout the hospital—a sickening odor that could be smelled far outside the hospital walls as well. The sewers did not function properly and were frequently backed up, spewing human waste into the hospital wards. War wounds accounted for only one death in six; most deaths were caused by diseases due to the unsanitary conditions in the hospital.

The army doctors gave the nurses five cramped rooms in which to work. They found the decaying corpse of a Russian general in one of those rooms. The central yard of the quad-rangle was a virtual dump inhabited by rats.

Each patient received a daily ration of only one pint of water. There were no cooking facilities, and only thirteen five-gallon copper pots were available for cooking the food to feed two thousand men. There were no vegetables; meat and flavored water were the patients' daily fare. The meat came from butchered animals, and the cooks would simply throw the meat chunks into water that wasn't hot enough to cook anything. As a result, that the patients were eating raw meat.

The soldiers came into the hospital with all kinds of wounds. They were ripped, torn, and mutilated. Many of their body parts were missing, and these were replaced with filthy, blood-clotted rags. The patients lay in rows on broken tile floors.

Florence observed the terrible conditions but did not complain. She took the words of a verse from Proverbs to heart: "A fool vents all his feelings, but a wise man holds them back" (Prov. 29:11, NKJV).

Sometimes the doctors wouldn't let the nurses get too involved in actual medical care, so the nurses would spend part of their time making slings, pillows, and mattresses in their efforts to help the ill and wounded. Florence was able to obtain vegetables from the local markets, and she got portable stoves that allowed the nurses to cook meals properly. She also bought tables and screens for the hospital. Many of these things were purchased from her private funds.

Charge of the Light Brigade

When wounded troops arrived from the Battle of Balaklava (where "the charge of the light brigade" had taken place), Florence and her nurses were ready. She wrote these words:

"On Thursday last, we had 1,715 sick and wounded in this hospital (among whom were 120 cholera patients) and 650 severely wounded in the other building, called the General Hospital, of which we also have charge, when a message came to me to prepare for 510 wounded on our side of the hospital, who were arriving from the dreadful affair...at Balaklava, where were 1,763 wounded and 442 killed besides 96 officers wounded and 38 killed....We had but half an hour's notice before they began landing the wounded. Between one and nine o'clock, we had the mattresses stuffed, sewn up, and laid down...the men washed and put to bed, and all their wounds dressed....Twenty-four cases [died] on the day of landing. We now have four miles of beds, and not eighteen inches apart....As I went my night-rounds among the newly-wounded that night, there was not one murmur, not one groan....These poor fellows bear pain and mutilation with an unshrinking heroism which is really superhuman, and die, or are cut up without a complaint....We have all the sick cookery now to do—and I have got in four men for the purpose....I hope in a few days we shall establish a little cleanliness. But we have not a basin, nor a towel, not a bit of soap, not a broom. I have ordered three hundred scrubbing brushes."[9]

In the face of such seemingly insurmountable odds many people would have despaired. Not Florence Nightingale; she persevered in her drive, compassion, and hard labor. She was able to work with the kitchen in such a way as to accommodate those patients who had special dietary needs. She and her nurses scrubbed the wards. They washed the patients and dressed their wounds regularly, and they emptied the chamber pots daily.

Out of her own money Florence purchased six thousand hospital gowns, two thousand pairs of socks, and hundreds of nightcaps, slippers, plates, cups, and utensils. She hired two hundred Turkish workers to restore the burned-out corridors, thus making room for an additional eight hundred patients.

Florence was passionate about what she knew God had called her to do, and she moved in unfeigned compassion among the sick and dying. She became compassion in action to those in need. She hired destitute women, many of whom were prostitutes, to serve as laundresses. She recommended a new system, which would require each bed to have tickets that would identify the patients' names and any dietary restrictions that applied to them. She wanted every patient to have his own bed with proper bedding.

Sometimes she would write letters home on behalf of the men and would send their meager wages to their families. Previously, many of them would squander their wages on alcohol. The army actually cut their wages when they got sick, and Florence assumed the role of their advocate in this matter as well as many others.

She introduced reading rooms into the hospital and secured the services of schoolmasters to give lectures to the men. Attendance at these lectures usually caused the halls to overflow.

One night, as Florence carried her lamp while doing her regular rounds, she found a man who was lying in the corridor. She realized that this soldier had never been attended to at all. In all the confusion he had been missed, and now he lay there dying. He could not make a sound, and she noticed that a bullet had penetrated one of his eyes. She later wrote, "Praise God! I found a surgeon, and the surgeon was able to save him."[10]

Awhile later, as she was out on the battlefield, she saw this man again. He had recuperated from the trauma and was back fighting on the field. He brought Florence a bouquet of flowers.

Whenever she went out among the men, they would rally around her. To them she was a true heroine, for she had given dignity, care, and honor to them. One of them said, "Behold the heroic daughter of England, a soldier's friend." Florence responded to this accolade with these words, "Give God the praise."[11] For her part, this valiant nurse had raised the image of the British soldier from a brawling low-life to a heroic working man.

Many days she would spend eight hours on her knees dressing wounds and comforting men who were scheduled for surgery. She had a wonderful presence about her that imparted peace to their hearts and calmed their nerves. She personally ministered to at least two thousand patients during the Crimean War.[12]

The mortality rate, which had been extremely high in the Barak Hospital, went below 10 percent under her care. Sometimes Florence herself worked so hard that she would pass out from sheer exhaustion. She always got back on her feet again, though, and continued her important service to the British soldiers.

When she had to return to England due to exhaustion and illness, Florence wrote these words about her service: "Oh, my poor men who endured so patiently, I feel I have been such a bad mother to you, to come home and leave you lying in your Crimean grave. Seventy-three percent in eight regiments during six months, from disease alone, who thinks of that now? But if I could carry any one point which would prevent any part of the recurrent of this, our colossal calamity, then I should have been true to the cause of those brave dead."[13]

Her extreme exhaustion led to a serious long-lasting illness. She developed a fever that was so high that the doctors had to shave her head in an effort to help release the heat from her body. For two weeks she suffered from delirium and bone-aching pain. She couldn't get out of bed, and this frustrated her greatly because she continued to sense the need of "her men."

By this time Florence Nightingale was famous, and even Queen Victoria worried about the state of her health. Eventually Florence was able to return to the hospital in Turkey, where she remained until the war was over two years and four months after it has started.

Four months after the peace treaty was signed, Florence returned home again. She hid herself away from the public because she didn't want any of the praise that she strongly felt belonged to God. About her service during the war and her feelings about longevity she said, "It matters little, provided we spend our lives to God, whether like our blessed Lord's they are concluded in three and thirty years, or whether they are prolonged to old age."

A Worker Approved

Paul, writing to Timothy, urged, "Study and do your best to present yourself to God approved, a workman [tested by trial] who has no reason to be ashamed, accurately handling and skillfully teaching the word of truth" (2 Tim. 2:15).

Florence Nightingale was such a worker. She had studied, was eager, and certainly did her utmost to present herself to God as one who was approved. She had been tested by trial and had no reason to be ashamed. Through her marvelous example we can learn so much, because she showed us what it means to be a worker approved by God.

After the war she got involved in several other matters, including writing, even though she was never completely well again and was often confined to her room. Nonetheless, she was a national heroine, and she began a campaign to improve the quality of care in military hospitals.

In October 1856, she had a long interview with Queen Victoria and her husband, Prince Albert. In 1859, she published two books that gave her opinions about the need for reform in hospital care: *Notes on Hospital* and *Notes on Nursing*. She raised funds to support her campaign to improve the quality of nursing. In 1860, Florence founded the Nightingale School and Home for Nurses at St. Thomas's Hospital in London. She also became involved in the training of nurses for employment in workhouses.

This valiant woman addressed the subject of women's rights in her book, *Suggestions for Thought to the Searchers after Religious Truths*. In this work she argued for the removal of restrictions that prevented women from having careers. Another book she wrote was titled *Suggestions for Thought to the Searchers after Truth among the Artizens of England,* which she kept revising until it seemed that God had spoken to her. He said, "You are here to carry out My program. I am not here to carry out yours." About this word from the Lord she wrote, "I must remember that God is not my private secretary!"

She served on the Indian Sanitary Commission by gathering documentation relating to the health and sanitary administration of the army in India. Her conclusion was that the death toll from disease in the Indian army was appallingly high, with sixty-nine out of every thousand dying annually due to a lack of sanitation.[14] Her findings resulted in the formation of the Army Medical College.

She revolutionized the public health system of India without ever leaving England, by writing pamphlet after pamphlet in which she used pie graphs to point out the most frequent causes for disease and death. She may well have been the first person to use such graphic displays to show statistics to people in an easy-to-understand manner. She was always careful to document her research.

Florence went on to study new designs for modern hospitals all over Europe. In Paris she found a revolutionary design in which separate units or pavilions made up one large hospital, and each pavilion was a light and airy self-contained unit. This design helped to minimize infections among the patients.

She began an anthology of mystical writings, which she called *Notes from Devotional Authors of the Middle Ages.* She believed that mystical prayer was for everyone, not just for monks, nuns, and priests. Prayer was a vital part of life for her, and it is clear from her writings that she relied on the power of prayer throughout her life. She wrote the manual *Notes for Nurses and a Set of Instructions for the Training of Nurses,* which emphasized the importance of nurses maintaining a daily schedule of prayer in their lives.

Her expertise gained her a reputation in America and Britain. The United States asked for Florence's help in establishing military hospitals for soldiers in the Civil War, and she was the first woman to receive the Order of Merit from the British government.

Due to continued overwork, her health continued to decline and she spent the last half of her life as an invalid. When she was sixty-five, she wrote this on Christmas Day: "Today, O Lord, let me dedicate this crumbling old woman to thee; behold, the handmaid of the Lord. I was thy handmaid as a girl, since then I have backslid."[15]

Florence Nightingale died at the age of ninety, and asked that the epitaph on her tombstone would read simply: "FN

1820 to 1910." She said that it would be a great honor for her to be buried in a casket that would be like those in which common soldiers are buried.[16]

Lioness Among Women

Florence Nightingale was a lioness among women—one whose faith, strength, and courage allowed her to live a compassion-acts lifestyle wherever she went.

We find a summation of her life and philosophy in these often-quoted words that she wrote long ago: "Life is a hard fight, a struggle, a wrestling with the principle of evil, hand to hand, foot to foot. Every inch of the way must be disputed. The night is given us to take breath, to pray, to drink deep at the fountain of power. The day, to use the strength which has been given to us, to go forth to work with it till the evening."

This is how compassion begins, how it grows, and how it keeps on going. So, drink deep at the fountain of power, and remember these words of Paul: "In conclusion, be strong in the Lord [draw your strength from Him and be empowered through your union with Him] and in the power of His [boundless] might" (Eph. 6:10).

Dear Heavenly Father, teach me to put You first in all that I do. Open my heart to serve the ones you put in my path. As I serve them, I serve you—my Redeemer and my Provider. May I look to You for guidance and not be satisfied with earthly wealth or status. My strength comes from you. May I use it to further Your kingdom in our world. In Jesus' name, amen.

+

Chapter 6

Gladys Aylward

REJECTED BY MAN, APPROVED BY GOD

(Michal Ann Goll)

I will be glad to be of service, sir," she grudgingly muttered, despite the fact her heart had just been ravaged by the harsh words spoken by the principal of the Women's Training Center of the China Inland Mission. Gladys Aylward was twenty-seven years old and, according to the staff of her mission preparatory school, too old to begin training to become a missionary in China. Sure, she knew her record wasn't the most impressive, but she was willing to do what was needed to get to China.

China. Her heart ached for China. While working as a parlormaid, she had attended a religious meeting, and by the end of the night, she had given her heart to Jesus. He gave it back to her with a deep-rooted love not only for Himself but also for the people of China.

She had read an article in a *Young Life Campaign* magazine about the millions of Chinese who had never heard the name "Jesus," and had felt an overwhelming compassion and desire to take action.[1] She tried to convince some of her Christian friends and relatives to take on the cause, but no one seemed very concerned. Surely if she asked her brother, he would understand her concern and move to China. Instead, he bluntly replied, "Not me! Why don't you go?"

Good question. Why didn't she go? If no one else would travel thousands of miles to a country she knew practically nothing about, she would be forced to go herself. She was told she would need to enlist in a certain missionary society and after completing training, she would be sent as a missionary to China. And now, sitting in the office of the man she had hoped would help fulfill her dreams, she was being told she was too old and too far behind the rest of the class. Instead of going to China, she was being offered another parlormaid position, this time caring for retired missionaries in need of a housekeeper.[2]

Questions flooded Gladys' mind. *Did I do something to upset God? Did I even hear God? Maybe I'm not called to China at all...*

Shaking off those thoughts, she held on to what she knew. God longed to embrace the Chinese people, and He wanted to use Gladys' hands and feet to do it. And in the meantime, if God wanted to use her hands and feet to serve an older missionary couple, who was she to stand in the way?

Early Missions Work

During Gladys' time in Bristol, England, caring for Dr. and Mrs. Fisher, she learned many valuable lessons from the couple's simple, extravagant faith in Jesus. While Gladys enjoyed the stories that filled the small house, she still longed to go and love the people of China. Next, she moved from Bristol to work for the Christian Association of Women and Girls, where she worked as a rescue sister. Each night she waded through the dark, gloomy streets near the docks, looking for girls that the sailors had made drunk, and took them back to the hostel. While she did enjoy this work and she knew God was using her, the faces of "her" people of China were etched in her heart and mind. She went to London to inquire of families in need of childcare—anything to earn her way to China. The responses she found were anything but helpful. Still, she refused to lose hope.

Diving into the Word for encouragement, she found herself under great conviction for her lack of faith and action concerning China. If she was so confident God had called her to China, why didn't she just act on it?

She read the story of Abraham. "Now the Lord had said unto Abram, Get thee out of thy country, and from thy kindred, and from thy father's house, unto a land that I will shew thee: and I will...make thy name great; and thou shalt be a blessing" (Gen. 12:1–2, KJV).

Then she read about Moses' absolute faith to obey God, to defy the might of Egypt and the despotism of Pharaoh. Nehemiah's life also called out to her. She saw that not only was he a butler of sorts and had to obey his employer, as she did—but he went. She heard a clear voice speak inside her soul asking if her God was the same one as the God of Nehemiah or not. God was building a whole series of confirmations that released a surge of courage that raced through her mind and spirit.[3] The issue was settled as far as she was concerned. She knew she had received her marching orders from heaven.

The Journey

Just as quickly as Gladys' heart surrendered to God's heart, provision and direction followed. She moved to London and began to save money for a ticket to China. But when Gladys arrived at Muller's Shipping Agency, she discovered the difficulty was not only in the price of the ticket but in the journey itself. The cheapest ticket would take her by rail through Europe, Russia, and Siberia to Tientsin in Northern China. At the time, war was raging between Russia and China. Fighting was over Manchurian soil and there was no guarantee she would get through safely. The clerk at the desk insisted traveling that distance was too great a risk, but Gladys knew in her heart she had to follow the heart of her God. That was the way to China.

Against the advice of the clerk on duty, she opened an account with the Muller's Shipping Agency with a deposit of three pounds toward a ticket to China, leaving forty-four pounds and ten shillings yet to pay. Within a few months, God had provided enough funds for her to travel to China. She worked extra hours, often taking on the serving for special socials and dinners. At one of these meetings, Gladys was introduced to a lady who shared interest in China and who told Gladys of her friend, Mrs. Lawson, an elderly missionary working in China who needed some "younger bones" to carry on her work. Gladys immediately wrote to Mrs. Lawson, offering her services. After a long wait, a reply arrived. If Gladys could travel to Tientsin, Mrs. Lawson would meet her. It was time.

She left Liverpool with two old battered suitcases that contained, among other things, a bedroll, a small alcohol stove, canned fish, crackers, boiled eggs, instant coffee, baked beans, and lots of tea. She tied on the outside of the suitcase a large pot and a kettle. She wore a bright orange dress and a huge fur overcoat with the sleeves cut out. Under her clothes she wore one of her mother's old corsets, into which she had sewn secret pockets to carry her train tickets, her passport, a fountain pen, her money (a grand nine pennies and two one-pound notes), and her Bible.[4] How she had waited for this day to come.

As the train jolted across the tracks, the day turned to night and the night back into day, and Gladys' excitement slowly dwindled into sadness and nervousness. She knew no one. She had no money. She was already tired.[5] What exactly was she thinking when this seemed like such a good idea?

She crossed the border into Manchuria and discovered fighting had intensified, blocking a crucial junction where Gladys had to change trains. After several stops, the lights in the train blackened and thundering gunfire broke the silence. She quickly grabbed her belongings and climbed onto the station platform, shivering in the bitter cold. The station seemed deserted, except for a few guards and uniformed officials who informed her she must walk through the howling wind and stinging cold to Chita, the previous stop on her route.

Gladys walked for several days to arrive back in Chita, stopping only to nap and nibble on the few crackers she had managed to save from the train. When she arrived in Chita, officials questioned her and attempted to persuade her to stay and work in Russia. While sitting in the train station, alone and cold, she questioned God and her own sanity for venturing on this journey alone, wondering if it would ever be worth it. But when she looked over and saw fifty people chained together by their hands and feet and being dragged onto trains to be taken to forced labor camps in Siberia, she knew her answer.

Of course it was worth it. She would pay any price and endure any suffering to get to China, the land where her heart longed to be so she could lavish hungry souls with the love of Jesus. With renewed energy and determination, she trekked on. After another detour, she found herself in Vladivostok, where an interpreter stole her passport and, with a manipulative smile and friendly voice, offered her a decent place to stay in a nearby hotel and a tour around the city. Although honored and appreciative at first, after a few days she began to feel anxious and ready to continue her journey to China. Unfortunately, the interpreter disagreed and insisted she stay. Since he still had her passport, she had no choice.

As she left the hotel in frustration, a woman appeared from behind the door and summoned her aside. In a hushed voice, the mysterious woman informed Gladys that the man who seemed hospitable had no plans of allowing Gladys to leave Russia and instructed her to quickly gather her things and wait for an old man to arrive at her door.

When a knock came a few hours later, Gladys jumped to her feet, anxious and nervous to open the door. The interpreter stood in the doorway, her passport in hand and a grim expression on his face. She grabbed the passport and slammed the door shut just in time. Looking at her passport, she saw it now read "Gladys Aylward, British subject; Profession: machinist." The mysterious woman was telling the truth; the interpreter had tried to change Gladys' passport to force her to stay in Russia.

Gladys was overwhelmed with gratitude for the angel God had sent to help her, but she knew she was not safe until she was out of Russia. In the early morning, another knock came at the door. An old man stood silently and held out his hand to carry Gladys' suitcase, leading her down a dark alley to the docks where they met the mysterious woman from the previous night. Again, her instructions were short and simple. Gladys must go down to the captain's hut and beg and plead, whatever it takes, to get on the boat for Japan.

With no valuables or money, Gladys had only one thing to offer the captain as a bargain: herself. Gladys agreed to become his prisoner, as long as they left Russia.[6]

In the darkest hour, Gladys knew she had a choice. She could forget why she had had traveled such a dangerous journey and become consumed with hopelessness and sadness at her terrible situation, or she could choose to believe. And she knew she must choose to believe in the goodness and faithfulness of her precious God and faithful King.

Touching the Soil

Eventually, the boat reached Japan and she found herself in the hands of the British Consulate. Relieved by the familiar language and comforting words of the officials, she was filled with joy and comfort. God was so faithful! He had once again delivered her from the enemy's hands and placed her in safe territory. On Sunday, November 5, 1932, three weeks after her departure from London, she stepped onto her last train ride into Tientsin to finally meet Mrs. Lawson.

Three days later, her feet touched the soil of a land she immediately called home. Her heart fell in love with the beautiful countryside, high mountains with snow-covered tops, and bright green and red trees. China.

When Gladys arrived in China, exhausted and dirty, she was relieved the journey was complete but nervous about the long-awaited meeting with Mrs. Lawson. Feeling unworthy and insignificant due to her unsightly appearance, she once again realized she had only one thing to offer: herself.

Mrs. Jeannie Lawson was from Scotland and rarely showed any sign of emotion. Rather harshly, Gladys was ushered into what was soon to be her new home. Gladys realized her hopes for a comfortable bed and warm bath were a bit premature when she walked into a dilapidated house where a cement floor was her bed. When asked where she should change clothes, Mrs. Lawson politely told her to sleep in her clothes with all her belongings within hand's reach—having her things close made them harder to steal. Gladys couldn't hide her frustration and anxiety, and again began questioning her sanity for moving to China.

Apparently, the news of her arrival had spread around town and she awoke with dozens of faces peering into the open windows. At any rate, she was grateful for the advice of Mrs. Lawson to sleep in her clothes.

Gladys was surprised at the bleak and poor conditions she and Mrs. Lawson faced on a daily basis. Ministry was not glamorous, she realized. Mrs. Lawson had little money; Gladys had nothing. So when Mrs. Lawson informed Gladys of her plans to transform the house into a working inn, Gladys was indeed relieved to know another source of income was on the way.

The inn was in Yangcheng, a little country Chinese village that sat on the ancient mule track where muleteers, the newsmen of North China, would travel on a regular basis. Excited about the opportunity to love and minister the good news of Jesus to the muleteers, Gladys was less than thrilled when she was assigned her task. Her job was to stand in the streets and, when the mules started to pass, grab the head of the first mule and drag him inside. Apparently, once this was done, the rest of the mules would follow and the muleteers would stay in the inn.

On her first day, Gladys stood shaking with fright as she waited for the mules to pass. Her first attempt failed miserably; the owner was so frightened he ran away. But soon Gladys perfected "the grab" and their home became known along the route as a clean inn where the foreign ladies told long stories at night, free of charge. The nighttime was Gladys' favorite part of the day because it was during these late hours Mrs. Lawson would begin to tell wonderful stories of their sweet Jesus. Gladys would listen carefully, trying to learn the language from Mrs. Lawson's stories, longing for the day it would be her turn to share.

Gladys completed all her daily tasks, no matter how mundane they seemed, to the best of her ability, knowing God could use even the smallest deeds of the day to His glory. She followed Mrs. Lawson faithfully, doing just as she was instructed and using any opportunity to learn more Chinese. Her days were often spent cleaning inside the inn, and during the night, Gladys could usually be found outside, cleaning and caring for the mules.

On weekends the duo would travel to villages, wait until crowds gathered to gaze in curiosity at the foreign ladies, and then begin to preach the gospel. The villagers would stare in amazement, as some had never before seen a white person. They stared especially at their feet. Chinese custom required all women to have their feet bound, so the "free feet" of Mrs. Lawson and Gladys always brought much attention.

Mrs. Lawson and Gladys were indeed a unique pair. Gladys' youthful energy was a definite contrast to the elderly Mrs. Lawson, who was strong in spirit but growing weaker physically by the day. What united the two was an unshakeable belief that God had called them to China; their love for the Chinese people was strong enough to fill any gap. Gladys often wondered what would happen to her if Mrs. Lawson died—would she be sent back to London or would she venture on alone?

Later on in the year, while Gladys was away from the inn,

Mrs. Lawson had a terrible accident; having fallen from the second-story balcony, she had lain outside for over a week, exposed to the weather, without any assistance from anyone. When Gladys returned, she found dear Mrs. Lawson lying on top of a pile of coal, where she had fallen. Gladys cared for her and nursed her, but it became evident she was not going to recover. Shortly before she passed into heaven, Mrs. Lawson whispered to Gladys, "God called you to my side, Gladys, in answer to my prayers. He wants you to carry on my work here. He will provide. He will bless and protect you."[7] Mrs. Lawson's funeral was the first Christian burial ever to be held in Yangcheng.[8]

Launching Out

Now alone, Gladys kept the inn running and held gospel meetings in the evenings. She traveled around to villages, caring for and giving medical aid as well as she could. Funds were extremely low, but that wasn't all. Mrs. Lawson had never told Gladys about a yearly tax due to the mandarin. This was a large amount, which Mrs. Lawson had paid out of her small monthly income. Now those funds were no longer available, and the payment was due.

Alone and tired, Gladys wondered how the she would meet the needs of her workers, her guests, and her beloved Chinese people. She felt weak and helpless, knowing God must truly work a miracle if she were to continue her work in China. Unable to bear the thought of closing the inn and leaving China, she knew the only place to go was to the feet of her Jesus and offer the only thing she had to give: herself.

She thought perhaps she should go and bow before the mandarin, but this idea presented several problems. Since Mrs. Lawson and Gladys were the first two foreigners to live in Yangcheng, there were no set rules as to how many times a foreigner should bow to the mandarin, or what she should say, or in what order either of these things should be done. Making just one mistake pertaining to proper protocol could be deadly, as the mandarin was the highest official in the district. The more she thought about this idea, the more she realized it just wouldn't be appropriate. She did not have any clothes suitable to seek an audience, having only her quilted blue trousers and jacket. No, there had to be some other way to deal with paying the taxes.

About a week later, Gladys had an unexpected surprise. The mandarin was seen coming to the inn. What could be the problem? Had she done something wrong? There was no time to make any preparations; she would just have to receive him with all the honor she held in her heart, and hope it would make the difference.

She bowed twice and waited, but the mandarin seemed focused on a mission. As he began speaking with her, the reason for his visit became clear. A new government had been formed in Nanking, and they had established a new law. This law addressed the ancient custom of foot-binding.

In those days, small feet were considered the ultimate in sexual appeal, and a woman's eligibility for a good marriage depended solely on this criterion. Depending on how affluent they were, Chinese families would bind the feet of their girl children with tight linen bandages while the little bones were soft and pliable, between the ages of three to seven years. The feet would slowly double over until the toes and front half of the foot were tucked underneath. By the time a girl was twelve or thirteen years old, her feet would be permanently doubled in half. Those who were less wealthy held off binding their daughter's feet for as long as they could so that their daughter could be useful longer around the house and the fields. Once her feet were bound, she would have difficulty getting around.

But now a new law challenged this custom. The new law required the mandarin to retain a foot inspector. This, in itself, presented two obstacles. First, the inspector could not be a man, as men were not allowed to look at a woman's feet. That meant the inspector had to be a woman. But all the women had already had their feet bound and they would not be able to travel on foot over mountains and rough roads to reach all the villages. These two issues narrowed down his search to the woman now standing in front of him. Who else was there who spoke the Yangcheng dialect, had unbound feet, and was a woman? There was only one in the entire Yangcheng district, and it was Gladys. She had made herself available, and now God was about to open to her a large field ready to be harvested.

The mandarin offered to pay her for this service, which would take care of the needed monies for the taxes. This would also give her the opportunity to tell every village throughout the entire district about Jesus, as well as help enforce the end of this terrible, torturous custom.

She found herself replying to him that if she took on this responsibility of representing his Excellency, she would speak of the love of God to everyone and lead as many to Jesus as she could. After thinking a few minutes, he in turn responded that if the women became Christians, they would want their daughters to have unbound feet like Gladys, and that would be a good thing.

This audience, which only took a few minutes, was the beginning of what would later become a crucial piece for the complete fulfillment of God's purposes in Gladys' life. As she went from village to village, house to house, she gathered each little girl in her arms and unbound the little feet that had turned white from lack of blood, sometimes with the toes already folded over. She gently massaged the feet until a pink color began to return and the toes began to uncurl, and then soundly threatened that if she came back and found the girl's feet bound again, that person would surely be put in prison. Many times she would be invited to the home of the elder of the village, where she would spend the night and tell stories about Jesus, her wonderful friend and Savior.

After several months, she had reached every village and every family, and unbound every girl's foot. She reported to the mandarin her progress, and he urged her to continue her rounds, making sure everyone was complying. Once the girls' feet were unbound, the parents often decided they were glad the old custom was abolished. This freed Gladys' time so that as she traveled, she was able to spend her time telling the people about Jesus. The villagers anticipated her visits, and as time passed, small bands of Christians began forming in the villages. Gladys visited the mandarin regularly, giving him updates on the region. He was greatly impressed with her work.

The Next Assignment

Some time later, another task was assigned to the "foot inspector." This time inmates in the prison had started a riot. They were killing each other. The mandarin, not knowing anyone else with as much courage or ability, summoned Gladys to the prison. Feeling totally overwhelmed and unprepared to face murderers and robbers, once she reluctantly arrived at the prison, she argued with the governor of the prison. What did she know about fighting, herself being a woman? Surely she would be killed.

The governor looked at her, and with a smile told her that she had been telling everyone that the living God lived inside her, so how could anyone kill her? Faced with the realization that this was the moment of truth, and that she had to stand on her faith in God, she silently prayed for God's protection and strength. She walked through the iron gate and down the pitch-black tunnel into the prison courtyard. She saw blood splattered everywhere as men lay dead or dying all over the ground. Others were running around with machetes, attacking each other.

In this den of violence, anger, and hate, Gladys stepped out of the shadows and ordered the men to stop at once, hand over the weapons, come together, and clean up the mess they had created. As she talked with them, she saw the desperation they were living in. Their bodies were so very thin, covered with oozing, open sores. They had lice in their hair, and what clothing they owned was completely worn out.

The men were dependent on their relatives to bring them food, and if they had no relatives, well, there was no food supplied for them. Gladys heard the stories of their situation and determined in her heart to do something about it. Who wouldn't riot living in such conditions? She corrected the governor of the prison, and told him things could not stay the way they were. She arranged for two old looms to be brought in so the prisoners could weave their own clothes, with local merchants supplying yarn. She begged for a miller's wheel so they could grind their own grain, and she taught the men how to breed rabbits for sale.

Within a few months of the riot, the men were dressed warmly and eating well. They gave her a new name: Ai-weh-deh, which means Virtuous One. Soon the name caught on, and everyone was calling her by her new name.

Serving the Children

As her understanding of the culture in this region grew, Ai-weh-deh became aware of the trade of buying and selling children. Her heart was continually being enlarged with every plight she discovered. How could she leave these little ones to suffer when she could do something on their behalf? One by one, she began adopting children. The first was Ninepence, followed by Less, Boa-Boa, Francis, and Lan Hsiang. Having adopted these children, she felt she needed to become a Chinese citizen so she would never be separated from them. The mandarin helped her fill out many papers, and in 1936 Gladys Aylward became the first foreign missionary to become a Chinese citizen.

The mandarin came to her regularly for help in solving problems. She started a school at the request of the prison governor. These were days of fulfillment and becoming really established in the region. However, there was a shadow of a problem in the distance that would soon knock on her door. War was about to envelope Yangcheng.

War

The Japanese had invaded Manchuria and set up their government there. But now they were moving farther into northeastern China. One morning in the spring of 1938, their beloved village was bombed. (Very few even knew what a bomb was.) Instantaneous devastation. The streets had huge craters in them, shops and houses were just piles of rubble. People were in shock.

Gladys gathered everyone together and set them to work. She had been working long hours caring for the wounded when she realized the mandarin was standing over her head. He had brought word to her that the Japanese were only about two days away from Yangcheng. The destruction that lay around them was only the beginning.

Several years of conflict between Japan and China followed. The conflict weakened the Chinese nationalist government to such an extent that the Communist government was able to slowly gain strength. During these years, regions went back and forth between Chinese and Japanese control.

Yangcheng was emptied on several occasions. The first time, under the counsel of Gladys, the prison governor, and the mandarin, everyone was told to leave the village, taking their food and livestock, giving the Japanese no reason to stay. Gladys, because of her extensive travels throughout the region, knew a perfect hiding place—Bei Chai Chuang. It was ideal, as there was no road that led to it, it was not on any map, and most importantly, the surrounding hills housed several large caves that were almost impossible to spot from the outside. This would become home to Gladys and her children for some time. Local people brought in food and supplies. A slow trickle of sick and wounded found their way to Gladys, knowing she would care for them. The cave was transformed into a hospital.

Things seemed to settle down in the beginning days of 1939, almost seeming normal. But once again the Japanese were on the move, and this time the Chinese felt the best way to defend the land was what they called a "scorched earth policy." They left nothing—no food, no crops, no buildings intact. Everything was destroyed or burned. This meant that the people of China would be left with nothing as well.

On the eve before all was destroyed, the mandarin held one last feast at his home and invited Gladys to attend. She was given the seat of honor. All the important people of Yangcheng were there. The mandarin stood and spoke of the many things Ai-weh-deh had done for him and for the people, going on for more than twenty minutes. Finally, at the end of his speech, he looked her directly in the eye, called her his dear friend, and told her he had seen all she was and all that she did. He wanted to become a Christian like her. How grateful Gladys was to the Lord, that He would do such a work in the mandarin's heart.

Places of Hiding

The war went on and on, and the scorched-earth policy left many in need. The caves continued to be a place of safety, and many came to receive the kindness and care of Gladys. When the number of children with her reached 150, Gladys stopped trying to keep count of them all. She endured many close calls with the Japanese. She ran through gunfire, wormed her way through wheat fields to escape, traveled along dangerous mountain trails, hid in clefts of rocks through the night, and endured a blow from the butt of a rifle on the side of her head, from which she never fully recovered.

She traveled from village to village, encouraging the churches there. Because of her extensive knowledge of the area, the general of the Chinese army requested any troop movement information she could give him. She was glad to do this, and knew she had become a spy for the land she loved. In the midst of all of this, she just kept doing what she could, many times not knowing if she would succeed. One of the prayers she had learned from Mrs. Lawson was, "If I die, let me not be afraid of death, but let there be a meaning, O God, in my dying."

In 1940 or 1941, she was interviewed by an American freelance journalist named Theodore White. Her compelling story was published in *Time* magazine and was read by millions of people, which unfortunately included the Japanese army. This ended up endangering her life and the lives of those under her care, as the Japanese put her on their wanted list—offering a reward for her, dead or alive.[9]

Two Hundred-Mile Journey

A possible option came up in regard to providing care for the two hundred children who were now in her care. It would require dividing them into two groups, and sending each group on a two-hundred-mile journey across the Yellow River to Sian in Shensi province. The first group, led by one of the new converts, made it safely, but on his way back to get the second group of children, this new convert, named Tsin Pen-kuang, was captured by the Japanese, robbed, and killed. The *Time* magazine article, by this time, had fallen into Japanese hands. Now the remaining children were at greater risk, just by being with her. What should she do? What could she do?

"Flee ye! Flee ye into the mountains! Dwell deeply in the hidden places, because the King of Babylon has conceived a purpose against you!" Her eyes read the verses from her Chinese Bible. Now she knew what she must do. She gathered all the children together, and they put on every piece of clothing they had and tied around their waists every spare pair of shoes they could find. Their shoes were made of cloth and would barely last a day on the rugged trails they would climb. Everyone had to carry his or her own bedroll. The oldest children were around fifteen years old, the youngest barely four years of age. She wrapped all the food she had in a rag, barely enough millet for two days' rations, and carried the old iron pot herself, to cook the millet in. No one had any idea how long a journey they were embarking on.

They slept in Buddhist temple courtyards, in the open air, in small homes, wherever they could find shelter. The older girls, whose feet had been bound previously, had great difficulty because of weakness and the abnormal bone formation. Finding enough food to feed one hundred children every day was more than just a challenge. They trekked over mountains with bruised and cut feet, the younger children in great despair, crying for lack of food and afraid. Gladys herself was dealing with a strange tiredness, a result of the rifle blow to her head. But she had to keep going.

Sometimes they sang hymns; sometimes they were silent, except for the children crying. There were many Japanese in the area, and they always had to be on the lookout, not knowing what they would do if they ran into any of them. There were the soldiers on the ground, but also they had to watch for the Japanese war planes that could suddenly appear. At times, they ran into Chinese soldiers, who sometimes carried sugar treats and food the children had not seen for months in Shansi province.

The soldiers were glad to share their provisions, missing their own beloved children. As food supplies dwindled, they picked twigs and leaves and brewed "tea"—anything to fill all the hungry stomachs. They had to cross the Yellow River, but when they arrived Gladys noticed that everyone had fled and there was no way to cross. All of the boats were gone. They sat by the river for four days before a Chinese soldier overheard them singing. There was one boat available to ferry the children across, but it would be very dangerous. If a Japanese war plane happened over the area at the wrong time, all would be lost. Gladys was slipping in and out of consciousness. Trying to stand up made her feel dizzy. They prayed, and after three trips across the river, all were safely on the other side. Relief was close at hand now—or was it?

The next morning they boarded the train and rode for three days only to discover that the bridge had been blown out. To get to Sian, they would have to climb over another mountain and catch another train on the other side. It would take four or five days to make this leg of the journey. How were they going to make it?

They got off the train and gazed at the steep grade of the climb before them. Gladys sat down on a rock and started to cry. One by one, they all joined in and cried together for several minutes till Gladys stopped, wiped her eyes on her sleeve, and told the children it was okay to cry but now it was time to move. It was time to sing, and time to march.

At every promise of being "almost there," there was always farther to go, it seemed, more miles to walk. "This train can't carry passengers. You can't stop here; no more refugees are being accepted." The delays were many. Finally, after three weeks or more, they arrived at Fufeng, a city that was still receiving refugees.

By this point Gladys, who didn't know it at the time, was suffering from fever, pneumonia, typhoid, and malnutrition. She delivered safely every child; not one of them had died or become seriously ill. She hardly knew who or where she was, and two days after getting the children to safety in an orphanage, she fell into a coma that lasted two weeks.

Need For Rest

It was time for recuperation. Gladys would require much time. She got stronger, and was able to resume her missionary work. She visited the head lama in Tibet, who told her they had been waiting for three years for someone to come who could tell them more about God. He showed her the

Scripture John 3:16: "For God so loved the world that He gave His only begotten Son," which had been glued to the wall. She preached to the Lamaist monks and prayed with them. She worked in a leper colony and preached in a local prison. Everywhere she went, many Chinese people were searching for the one true God.

She witnessed among university students the ugliness of the communist regime, as they were given the choice to either support the communist government or not. One by one, these fiery students, who knew of a higher allegiance, having made their declaration for Jesus, were promptly shoved to their knees and beheaded, right there on the spot.

Gladys went back to England for a while to recuperate some more from the physical rigors she had endured. She was not prepared for how famous she had become. She traveled to many places, using her notoriety to call Christians to pray for China and send relief to the Chinese people. Hollywood made a movie about her life called *Inn of the Sixth Happiness*, and the big London newspapers interviewed her. She was introduced to heads of state, met Queen Elizabeth, and worked with the many refugees who streamed into England.[10]

Desire to Go Home

After ten years in England, she traveled back "home." Entry into mainland China was not allowed, and her Chinese citizenship was not honored at this time, so in 1957 she landed in Formosa (modern-day Taiwan). She picked up her life where she had left off. Her heart was full, and her hands were never empty.

On New Year's Day in 1970, Gladys simply did not wake up. She was sixty-seven years old, and her heart just stopped beating. Beside her bed was a newborn baby, sleeping peacefully. The baby had been abandoned and brought to Ai-weh-deh, where it had been received with open, loving arms.

Memorial services were held around the world for this amazing woman, and over a thousand people attended her funeral service in Taipei. Gladys' body was buried on a hill-top at Christ's College in Taipei, with her tomb facing the Chinese mainland.

> Father, I come to You in the name of Jesus. I pray that I would know Your voice and Your Word so well that I would be totally transformed by Your Word and become a living epistle to the world. Oh Lord, may I be so in love with You that no obstacle would keep me from doing all I can do for Your name's sake. May man's opinion not sway or affect my focus and determination to do all You have deposited in my heart. May I always remember that it is Your approval, not that of other people, that counts. In Jesus' name, amen.

Chapter 7

———

Mother Teresa
THE HUMBLE ROAD

(Michal Ann Goll)

If you asked people, "Who was the most compassionate person of the twentieth century?" I'm sure many would answer without hesitation, "Mother Teresa." She moved in compassion among the poor in her beloved Calcutta, India, and among the rich and famous around the world as well. She was a flesh-and-blood example of what compassion looks like, and she seemed to exhibit the qualities of humility and love wherever she was.

Indeed, she obviously took joy from her service to others and this seemed to fill her heart with peace. This was reflected in her radiant, smiling countenance.

There is much we can learn from Mother Teresa, and I feel as if I have actually gotten to know her as I researched and wrote this chapter. I hope you are inspired as you read these pages about her life and ministry.

Mother Teresa of Calcutta (Agnes Gonxha Bojaxhiu) was born on August 27, 1910, in Skopje, which is in modern

Macedonia. Her family was of Albanian descent, and she was the youngest of three children. Her father was a builder.

At the age of twelve, Agnes strongly felt the call of God on her life, and she knew that she was destined to become a missionary. The overarching desire of her life from then on was to spread the love of Jesus Christ, particularly among the poor, the sick, and the outcasts of society.

When she was eighteen years old, Agnes left home to join the Sisters of Loretto, an Irish community of nuns who managed mission schools in India. As a novice in this order, she took the name of Sister Teresa. She served her novitiate in Dublin, and after several months of training was sent to India. On May 25, 1931, she took her initial vows as a nun.

From 1931 to 1948, Sister Teresa taught at St. Mary's High School in Calcutta. While there, she was moved with deep compassion for the poor and suffering people she saw outside the walls of the convent. Thousands of destitute people lived there with little hope that the basic necessities of life—food, shelter, health, cleanliness, and income—would ever be theirs.

In 1946, Sister Teresa developed a suspected case of tuberculosis. To get her out of the crowded city into the mountain air, she was sent by train to the village of Darjeeling, in the foothills of the Himalayas. While sitting on the train, she heard God speaking to her and telling her that He wanted her to serve Him "among the poorest of the poor."

Soon, she recovered from her illness and received permission to leave her order. She moved to Calcutta's slums to set up her first school for slum children in an open-air mission. She had no funds for this work, so she had to depend on faith in God's provision. Clearly, she knew the truth of this Scripture: "And without faith it is impossible to please

God, because anyone who comes to him must believe that he exists and that he rewards those who earnestly seek him" (Heb. 11:6, NIV).

Before long, volunteers joined with her, and people who saw what she was doing began to provide financial support for her fledgling ministry. This allowed her work and ministry to grow.

Calcutta, India

Calcutta (Kolkata) is the capital of the Indian state of West Bengal in eastern India. It is the fourth largest city in India, with a population that currently exceeds five million.

After India declared its independence from Great Britain in 1947, the city went through an extended period of economic stagnation and many of its inhabitants were the "poorest of the poor." The city's port had been bombed by the Japanese twice during World War II. Millions had starved to death during the Bengal famine of 1943. In 1946, demands for the creation of a Muslim state had led to massive violence in the city, and more than two thousand people had died.

When the subcontinent was divided between India and Pakistan in 1947, a flood of over one million destitute refugees poured into Calcutta. Most of these people were Hindus who had no concept of a personal God who was their heavenly Father. The majority of people who lived in Calcutta during the 1940s lived in the worst possible conditions of extreme hunger, deprivation, squalor, and filth.

Sister Teresa went through these great trials with the Indian people, so she knew how intense their suffering and hardships were. She gathered the city's "throwaway children" from rubbish heaps. Many were orphans. She explained, "We do our best to nurse them back to life."[1]

This valiant nun could see the life of Jesus in every child and adult, and she approached each one as if he or she was the Lord himself. She was their servant, an obedient follower of the One who said:

> For I was hungry, and you gave Me something to eat; I was thirsty, and you gave Me something to drink; I was a stranger, and you invited Me in; I was naked, and you clothed Me; I was sick, and you visited Me [with help and ministering care]; I was in prison, and you came to Me [ignoring personal danger]. (Matt. 25:35–36)

When Jesus' disciples asked Him when it was that they had done these things, He said, "Truly I tell you, whatever you did for one of the least of these brothers and sisters of mine, you did for me" (Matt. 25:40, NIV).

Sister Teresa gave food to the hungry, hospitality to the strangers, clothes to the naked, and healing and practical help to the ill. She explained, "In the slums we are the light of God's kindness to the poor. To the children, to all who suffer and are lonely, [we] give always a happy smile...not only [our] care but also [our] heart."[2]

In spite of its poverty, violence, and bloodshed, Calcutta came to be known as "the City of Joy," and Sister Teresa was able to help turn suffering into joy for many people who lived there.

Saint of the Gutter

On October 7, 1950, Sister Teresa was given permission by the Holy See to found a new order of Catholic nuns—the Missionaries of Charity. She was now Mother Teresa of Calcutta, the Mother Superior of this new order.[3]

She saw the order's primary task as being the provision of love and care for needy persons who had no one to help them.[4] Mother Teresa described their mission as follows: "...[to care for] the hungry, the naked, the homeless, the crippled, the blind, the lepers, all those people who feel unwanted, unloved, uncared for throughout society, people that have become a burden to the society and are shunned by everyone."[4]

The Missionaries of Charity began with only twelve members in Calcutta. Today there are more than four thousand nuns in the order throughout the world, and they minister to orphans, AIDS victims, refugees, the blind, the disabled, the aged, alcoholics, the poor, victims of natural disasters, and the hungry. They can be found working in Asia, Africa, Latin America, North America, Poland, and Australia.

Mother Teresa always emphasized service to others. She believed and followed these words of Jesus: "And whosoever of you shall be the chiefest, shall be servant of all" (Mark 10:44, KJV). She became a leader because she was a servant, and her Sisters of Charity truly are the servants of all. These are some of the reasons why Mother Teresa became known as "the saint of the gutter."

Her Spiritual Life

Pope John Paul II admired Mother Teresa, and he said that she was one of the greatest missionaries of the twentieth century. He explained, "The Lord made this simple woman who came from one of Europe's poorest regions a chosen instrument (see Acts 9:15) to proclaim the gospel to the entire world, not by preaching, but by daily acts of love towards the poorest of the poor. A missionary with the most universal language: the language of love that knows no bounds or exclusion and has no preferences other than for the most for-saken....Where did Mother Teresa find the strength to place herself completely at the service of others? She found it in prayer and in the silent contemplation of Jesus Christ..."[5]

In his first encyclical, Pope Benedict XVI echoed John Paul's observations by stating, "In the example of Blessed Teresa of Calcutta we have a clear illustration of the fact that time devoted to God in prayer not only does not detract from effective and loving service to our neighbour but is in fact the inexhaustible source of that service."[6]

Angel of Mercy

Mother Teresa was also known as an "angel of mercy" to the poor. This is an apt description of her work, for an angel is a messenger, one who is always ready to come to the aid of others. She opened Nirmal Hriday ("Pure or Immaculate Heart"), a home for the dying, in 1952. This hostel became the focal point of her ministry for a couple of years. The government leaders of Calcutta gave her the use of a building for this purpose.

Writer Eileen Egan describes her work there as follows:

I watched Mother Teresa as she sat on the parapet next to the low pallets of men, patting their heads or stroking their stick-like arms, murmuring to each one. Sometimes only the eyes seemed alive in men whose skin was drawn so tightly that the skull seemed struggling to burst through. Some were even smiling, as though amazed to be alive. It was the same in the women's hall. Seeing me, they held out their wasted hands to me, searching for human consolation. I turned away in fear and shame. I wondered how she could face day after day caring for those who were brought in covered with the filth and spittle of the gutter. Mother Teresa explained that her work and the work of the Sisters called for them to see Jesus in everyone, including the men and women dying in the gutter.[7]

Mother Teresa said that in the earlier days of their ministry they did little planning. They simply responded to the needs, and she stated that God showed them what to do. She said, "Keep giving Jesus to your people not by words, but by your example, by your being in love with Jesus, by radiating his holiness and spreading his fragrance of love everywhere you go. Just keep the joy of Jesus as your strength. Be happy and at peace. Accept whatever he gives—and give whatever he takes with a big smile. You belong to him."[8]

I love this simple statement of faith. We should never forget that we are God's property, as Paul pointed out to the Corinthians: "You were bought with a price [you were actually purchased with the precious blood of Jesus and made His own]. So then, honor and glorify God with your body" (1 Cor. 6:20). Knowing that we are no longer our own, that we have been bought with a price, helps to clarify many things in our lives. It helps us to see what God wants us to do. It makes us realize that we do not have to do anything in our own strength.

Pure Religion

The apostle James wrote, "Pure and unblemished religion [as it is expressed in outward acts] in the sight of our God and Father is this: to visit and look after the fatherless and the widows in their distress, and to keep oneself uncontaminated by the [secular] world" (Jas. 1:27). Mother Teresa's life was characterized by this kind of "external religious worship."

After opening her free hospice for the poor, Mother Teresa opened a home for lepers, which she called Shanti Nagar ("City of Peace"). Then she opened an orphanage, Shishu Bhavan. She became a true mother to the precious children who lived there.

About her work in the orphanage, Mother Teresa wrote:

> One of the abandoned children we had in our Shishu Bhavan I gave to a very high-class and rich family. After a few months I heard that the child had become very sick and completely disabled. So I went to that family and said, "Give me back the child and I will give you a healthy child." The father looked at me and said, "Take my life first, then take the child." He loved the child from his heart. In Calcutta, every night we send word to all the clinics, to all the police stations, to all the hospitals, "Please do not destroy any children; we will take them all." So our house is always full of children. There is a joke in Calcutta: "Mother Teresa is always talking about family planning and abortion, but every day she has more and more children."[9]

How did Mother Teresa learn to be such a giving parent? She developed her parenting skills by getting to know her heavenly Father. She often spoke of His tenderness to her and quoted these verses from the prophet Isaiah:

> But now, thus says the Lord, who created you, O Jacob, and He who formed you, O Israel: Fear not, for I have redeemed you; I have called you by your

name; you are Mine. When you pass through the waters, I will be with you; and through the rivers, they shall not overflow you. When you walk through the fire, you shall not be burned, nor shall the flame scorch you. (Isa. 43:1–2, NKJV)

She knew that God was her loving heavenly Father and that He would always be with her. She stood upon His promise that He would never leave her nor forsake her. It was obvious to all who knew her that she knew God personally and intimately.

Mother Teresa understood that God had adopted her into His family, that she was His child. Like Paul, she believed, "For all who are allowing themselves to be led by the Spirit of God are sons of God. For you have not received a spirit of slavery leading again to fear [of God's judgment], but you have received the Spirit of adoption as sons [the Spirit producing sonship] by which we [joyfully] cry, 'Abba! Father!'" (Rom. 8:14–15).

I'm sure this is why she respected life so much and was adamantly opposed to abortion. She always encouraged people to adopt children so that they could experience family love, nurturing, and support. She frequently spoke against abortion and artificial contraception. When she accepted the Nobel Peace Prize in 1979, she said, "I feel the greatest destroyer of peace today is abortion, because it is a direct war, a direct killing—direct murder by the mother herself.... Because if a mother can kill her own child—what is left [but] for me to kill you and you kill me—there is nothing between."[10]

To her, abortion was infanticide—a blatant disregard for God's gift of life—and in 1994, at the National Prayer

Breakfast in Washington, D.C., she said, "Please don't kill the child. I want the child. Please give me the child. I am willing to accept any child who would be aborted and to give that child to a married couple who will love the child and be loved by the child."[11]

This is complete compassion—a willingness to do all that could be done for those in need. Her offer to take any unwanted child had no limits; it was an open-ended and heartfelt invitation from a true mother who knew how much Jesus loves the little children. Her offer reminds me of what Jesus said: "Leave the children alone, and do not forbid them from coming to Me; for the kingdom of heaven belongs to such as these" (Matt. 19:14).

Forgiveness

Mother Teresa believed in the importance of forgiveness. She said:

> I once picked up a woman from a garbage dump and she was burning with fever; she was in her last days and her only lament was: "My son did this to me." I begged her: "You must forgive your son. In a moment of madness, when he was not himself, he did a thing he regrets. Be a mother to him, forgive him." It took me a long time to make her say: "I forgive my son." Just before she died in my arms, she was able to say that with a real forgiveness. She was not concerned that she was dying. The breaking of the heart was that her son did not want her. This is something you and I can understand."[12]

Forgiveness is an important part of compassion, for it is only as we are able to empathize with and understand the person who has wronged us that we will be able to forgive them and find peace for ourselves. Paul writes, "Be kind and helpful to one another, tender-hearted [compassionate, understanding], forgiving one another [readily and freely], just as God in Christ also forgave you" (Eph. 4:32). This is the lifestyle of compassion, and these qualities are desperately needed in society today.

Mother Teresa expressed her feelings about life and her relationship with Jesus Christ in the following poem:

> He is the Life that I want to live,
> He is the Light that I want to radiate.
> He is the Way to the Father.
> He is the Love with which I want to love.
> He is the Joy that I want to share.
> He is the Peace that I want to sow.
> Jesus is everything to me.
> Without Him, I can do nothing.[13]

Something Beautiful for God

In 1969, Malcolm Muggeridge produced a documentary about Mother Teresa's life titled *Something Beautiful for God*. In 1971, he wrote a book with the same title. These two works helped to spread the name of Mother Teresa around the world. She became the best-known missionary in the world, and people everywhere respected her life and her work.

She received many accolades and awards, including the first Pope John XXIII Peace Prize (1971), the Kennedy Prize (1971), the Albert Schweitzer International Prize (1975), the Balzan Prize for humanity, peace, and brotherhood among peoples (1978), the United States Presidential Medal of Freedom (1985), the Congressional Gold Medal (1994), honorary citizenship of the United States (1996), the Nobel Peace Prize

(1997), and honorary degrees from numerous colleges and universities.

Hers was a life well-lived, and she became "something beautiful for God" indeed. In 1999 a Gallup poll found that Mother Teresa was the most admired person of the twentieth century.

In 1982, Mother Teresa was successful in persuading the Israelis and Palestinians to stop shooting long enough to enable her organization to rescue thirty-seven retarded children from a hospital in Beirut. The love and compassion she exhibited is needed in the Middle East today.

In the 1980s and 1990s her health began to decline. She suffered her first heart attack in 1983 while she was visiting Pope John Paul II in Rome. She received a pacemaker after her second heart attack in 1989. When she was in Mexico in 1991, she developed pneumonia, which led to further heart problems. In the face of her deteriorating health, Mother Teresa offered to resign as the head of the Missionaries of Charity, but the sisters had a vote, and all of them voted for her to remain in leadership, so she continued on with her ministry.

In 1996, Mother Teresa suffered a fall that caused her to break her collar bone. In August of that same year she suffered from malaria, and the left ventricle of her heart failed, causing her to undergo heart surgery. On March 13, 1997, she stepped down as the head of her order, and she died later that year, on September 5, 1997. She was eighty-seven years old.

At the time of her death there were more than 4,000 sisters serving with the Missionaries of Charity around the world. In addition, 300 brothers had become associated with the order, along with over 100,000 lay volunteers. These devoted servants of God operated 610 missions in 123 countries, including hospices, homes for people with HIV/AIDS, leprosy and tuberculosis sanitariums, soup kitchens, children and family counseling programs, orphanages, and schools.

This humble woman who came from an obscure village in Macedonia had risen to become the most respected woman in the world because she was faithful to the call God gave to her. In devoting her life to serving others, she became a role model of compassion for all of us to follow.

Peace and Joy

Mother Teresa has often been compared to Saint Francis of Assisi, the thirteenth-century friar who found his joy in serving others. She loved his lifestyle of compassion, poverty, and service, and she learned a great deal from him.

She was fond of praying (and living) St. Francis' well-known prayer:

> Lord, make me an instrument of your peace;
> Where there is hatred, let me sow love;
> Where there is injury, pardon;
> Where there is despair, hope.
> O Divine Master, grant that I might seek
> Not so much to be consoled, as to console;
> To be understood, as to understand;
> Not so much to be loved, as to love another.
> For it is in giving that we receive;
> It is in pardoning that we are pardoned;
> It is in dying that we are born to eternal life.

Mother Teresa was an instrument of peace in the world. The former Secretary-General of the United Nations, Javier Perez de Cuellar, said about her: "She is the United Nations. She is peace in the world."

"Do small things with great love"

One of Mother Teresa's best-known mottos is, "Do small things with great love." This simple but profound advice is what the world needs today. She also said, "Never forget you are co-workers of Jesus." These two quotations form the framework of Mother Teresa's life and ministry, and, when we apply them to our own lives, we will see exciting changes taking place in our life and ministry.

As we let the peace and compassion of Jesus fill our hearts, we follow the trail that Mother Teresa has blazed, and we walk in the footsteps of Jesus: "To this you were called, because Christ suffered for you, leaving you an example, that you should follow in his steps" (1 Pet. 2:21, NIV).

In conclusion, I offer a simple quote from Mother Teresa that seems to reveal the secret of her success in service to others. I ask you to reflect on her words and apply them to your life: "When there is a call within a call, there is only one thing to do, to say 'yes' to Jesus. That's all. If we belong to him, he must be able to use us without consulting us....I had only to say a simple 'yes.'"[15]

> Dear Heavenly Father, in Jesus' name I come before You to offer my life to help Your children, young and old, in whatever way is right and lovely in Your eyes. May I follow the example of Jesus when He ministered to them out of love and compassion. Your example is the only example I need; Your love is the only love I need to share with others. It is pure and holy, nourishment to body and spirit. In the precious name of Jesus, amen.

—✝—

Chapter 8

LITTLE WOMEN— BIG GOD

(Michal Ann Goll)

This chapter focuses on the lives and ministries of five little ladies who became great women of God: Amy Carmichael, Katharine Drexel, Phoebe Palmer, Hannah More, and Elizabeth Fry. Each one of their hearts was filled with compassion, and they spent their lives in service to God by helping others.

As I have studied their lives and writings, I have been deeply stirred to become more like them, for these women lived close to God and shared His life with the people He brought to them. I'm sure you will be impressed, as I was, by their uncompromising devotion to the Lord. God called each of these women to acts of compassion and uncommon valor. They were women after God's own heart, ladies of character who lived their lives in sold-out commitment to the Father.

As you read their stories, may you respond to His call as well, for He is looking for those who will obey Him by going forth into the whitened harvest fields during these last days of human history.

Abandoned to God—Amy Carmichael

Amy Carmichael was born on December 16, 1867, in Millisle, a small village in Northern Ireland. As its name implies, this was a place of mills (flour mills), where Amy's father acquired considerable wealth. Unfortunately, her father died when Amy was eighteen years old, and this resulted in financial uncertainty for the Carmichael family, which was subsequently forced to move to Belfast.

Amy was the oldest of seven children. One wintry Sunday morning, as the family was returning home from the Presbyterian church they attended, Amy and her two brothers saw an old woman who was carrying a large bundle. All the children wanted to help her, but they felt somewhat embarrassed about asking her if they could help. Nonetheless, they went to her aid.

Amy writes, "This meant facing all the respectable people who were, like ourselves, on their way home. It was a horrid moment. We were only two boys and a girl, and not at all exalted Christians. We hated doing it. Crimson all over (at least we felt crimson, soul and body of us) we plodded on, a wet wind blows in about us, and blowing, too, the rags of that poor old woman, till she seemed like a bundle of feathers and we unhappily mixed up with them."[1]

As they kept walking, they came to a beautiful Victorian fountain. Just as they were passing this fountain, Amy heard a voice that was speaking the words of a Scripture verse: "Now if any man build upon this foundation gold, silver, precious stones, wood, hay, stubble; every man's work shall be made manifest; for the day shall declare it, because it shall be revealed by fire; and the fire shall try every man's work of what sort it is. If any man's work abide..." (1 Cor. 3:12–14, KJV).

Startled by this message, Amy turned around to see who

had spoken it to her, but no one was there, and all she heard then was the bubbling and splashing of the fountain and a few distant passersby who were talking with each other.[2] She knew then that God was calling her to "settle some things with Him."[3] Prior to this she had been primarily preoccupied with her social life.

The death of her father caused Amy to reevaluate her values and beliefs, and she began to think seriously about her future and God's plan for her life. As a result, she began to work in an inner-city mission in Belfast.

The Carmichaels traveled to Cumbria County, England, in order to attend a Keswick Conference in England's Lake District. The convention had begun a decade or so earlier as an important gathering of evangelical Christians. It was the center of what came to be known as the Higher Life Movement in Great Britain. Personal holiness was the major emphasis of this movement.

Amy Carmichael was greatly influenced by her experience there. She writes, "The hall was full of a sort of gray mist, very dull and chilly. I came to that meeting half hoping, half fearing. Would there be anything for me?...the fog in the Hall seemed to soak into me. My soul was in a fog. Then the chairman rose for the last prayer...'O Lord, we know Thou art able to keep us from falling.' Those words found me. It was as if they were alight. And they shone for me."[4]

This was the moment when Amy realized that she must dedicate her whole life to the Lord Jesus Christ, who had given His life for her. In her heart of hearts, she understood that she had to do the same in return and give her all to Him.

Amy began to realize that she had to die to the self-life in order to follow the Lord's leading. She knew the meaning of

Paul's words, "I am crucified with Christ: nevertheless I live; yet not I, but Christ liveth in me: and the life which I now live in the flesh I live by the faith of the Son of God, who loved me, and gave himself for me" (Gal. 2:20, KJV). Nothing but complete surrender to Jesus could satisfy her now, and she determined to give her life in total abandonment to Him.

In 1887, Amy heard a speech by China Inland Mission founder Hudson Taylor, and his compelling message ignited her passion for missions. In 1893, she left for Japan with the support of the Keswick Convention, but this initial introduction to foreign missionary service was a big disappointment to her, because she felt there was little difference between the missionaries she worked with there and people in the world.

She wrote, "...we are here just what we are at home—not one bit better—and the devil is awfully busy...There are missionary shipwrecks of once-fair vessels."[5] Amy wanted more of God, and her desire to live a holy life before Him pushed her away from her work in Japan. She decided to return home, but on her way back to England, she stopped in Ceylon to help care for a sick family friend.

Upon returning home, she continued seeking God and His will for her life. After less than a year back home, she decided to return to the mission field. This time she went to India—the place God had picked for her. It was 1895 and she was commissioned by the Church of England Zenana Missionary Society to go to Dohnavur, India, where she subsequently served for fifty-six years without a furlough.

In time, Amy Carmichael founded the Dohnavur Fellowship for Girls, which was a ministry devoted to rescuing girls whose families had dedicated them to become temple prostitutes. Through her ministry, more than a thousand children were rescued from abuse and neglect. The children called her "Amma," which means "mother" in the Tamil language, and Amy truly became a mother to them.

She wrote:

> There were days when the sky turned black for me because of what I heard and knew was true....Sometimes it was as if I saw the Lord Jesus Christ kneeling alone, as He knelt long ago under the olive trees....And the only thing that one who cared could do was to go softly and kneel down beside Him, so that He would not be alone in His sorrow over the little children.[6]

Amy Carmichael was a devout woman of prayer, and her life was characterized by total commitment, all-out compassion, obedience, and selflessness. One of her most heart-felt prayers, a prayer that became the theme of her life, was expressed in the following poem:

> O Father, help, lest our poor love refuse
> For our beloved the life that they would choose,
> And in our fear of loss for them, or pain,
> Forget eternal gain.
> Show us the gain, the golden harvest there
> For corn of wheat that they have buried here;
> Lest human love defraud them and betray,
> Teach us, O God, to pray.
> Teach us to pray, remembering Calvary,
> For as the Master must the servant be;
> We see their face set toward Jerusalem,
> Let us not hinder them.
> Teach us to pray; O Thou who didst not spare
> Thine own Beloved, lead us on in prayer;

Purge from the earthly, give us love Divine,
Father, like Thine, like Thine.[7]

Amy Carmichael wrote thirty-five books, many of which continue to inspire people around the world today. She was crippled by a fall in 1931, and four years later she became bedridden. She remained an invalid until her death in 1951, and she was buried in her beloved Dohnavur.

For more than fifty years Amy's overarching goal in life was: "To save children in moral danger; to train them to serve others; to succor the desolate and the suffering; to do anything that may be shown to be the will of our heavenly Father, in order to make His love known, especially to the people of India."

The "Millionaire Nun"—Katharine Drexel

Katharine Mary Drexel was born in Philadelphia, Pennsylvania, in 1858. She was the second daughter of a wealthy Philadelphia banker, Francis Martin Drexel, and his wife, Hannah Langstroth. Her mother died approximately one month after Katharine was born.

Katharine's sister, Elizabeth, was three years older than she. When her father remarried, another sister, Louise, was born in 1863. Francis's new wife, Emma Bouvier, became a very devoted mother to Katharine and her sisters.

The Drexel girls did not go to school; they were home-schooled by governesses. Nonetheless, Katharine was well-educated and her natural intelligence became obvious to all when she was very young. As she grew up she was able to travel extensively with her family, and this broadened Katharine's understanding of the world and its people. On one trip to the Southwest, Katharine saw firsthand the deprivation of Native Americans and was appalled to see the deplorable conditions in which they lived.

This caused her to resolve to do something to help the poor when she got older, and this may well have been the time when her heart for missions began to develop. Around this same time, she also began to become deeply concerned about the plight of African-Americans.

Katharine's parents instilled in their children the concept that wealth was a gift from God that He wanted them to share with others.[8] Jesus said, "freely ye have received, freely give" (Matt. 10:8, KJV), and this was Katharine's approach to life and ministry when she became a nun in 1889. She entered the Sisters of Mercy convent in Pittsburgh, Pennsylvania, and while preparing for her vows, she began to sense that God was calling her to a ministry to the poor.

Katharine had a personal visit with Pope Leo XIII in 1883. She asked him what could be done for the American Indians and blacks in the United States. The pope answered, "Daughter, why don't you become a missionary?" His question stirred something deep inside her; she felt she had heard God's challenge, and she began to weep.[9]

As a result, she began to envision a new order of nuns who would serve Native Americans and African-Americans in particular. When she returned to America, she consulted with her spiritual director, Bishop James O'Conner. He advised her to start her own religious community.

The new order—the Sisters of the Blessed Sacrament for Indians and Colored People—was founded on February 12, 1891, and Katharine Drexel took the name of Mother Katharine Drexel. Because she was a multimillionaire and had taken the vow of poverty, Archbishop Patrick Ryan of

Philadelphia reminded her that she needed to be willing to surrender her funds to the Lord's work.

From then on, she lived a very austere life, using money for herself only to provide for the basic necessities of life. Though she was rich, she voluntarily became a poor woman who ministered to the poor, much like Jesus Himself:

> For you know the grace of our Lord Jesus Christ, that though He was rich, yet for your sakes He became poor, that you through His poverty might become rich. (2 Cor. 8:9, NKJV)

Using her money for God, Mother Katharine began by building a convent in Bensalem, Pennsylvania, not far from her native Philadelphia. In her lifetime she freely gave nearly twenty million dollars from her parents' estate to the poor. She established sixty missions to provide education for American Indians and blacks, and she and her sisters dedicated their lives completely to the welfare of these disadvantaged people.[10]

Along the way, Mother Katharine and her sisters encountered great opposition, particularly from people with racial prejudices. She never wavered in the face of conflict, however, and eventually won the respect of many people, even former enemies. She always stood stalwartly for justice, mercy, and peace.

Katharine was a woman who believed in the power of prayer. She asked God to intervene in the lives of Native Americans and African-Americans and to stem the tide of racism in the United States. Though the Civil War had ended a few decades earlier, she realized that many blacks were still not free and had to live in substandard conditions as sharecroppers and menial laborers.

She recognized that American Indians and blacks were denied the rights of full citizenship and equality in many places and that those who were able to attend school received poor educations. As a result, she developed "a compassionate urgency to help change racial attitudes in the United States."[11]

In 1915, Mother Katharine was responsible for the establishment of Xavier University in New Orleans, which was then the only Catholic university for blacks in America.

Throughout her long and devoted life, Katharine Drexel held true to the stated goals of the order she founded:

1. The primary object which the Sisters of this religious congregation purpose to themselves is their own personal sanctification.
2. The secondary and special object of the members of the congregation is to apply themselves zealously to the service of Our Lord…by endeavoring to lead the Indian and Colored races to the knowledge and love of God, and so make them living temples of our Lord's divinity.[12]

The Roman Catholic Church canonized Mother Katharine Drexel in 2000. In her lifetime of service to God and His Church she accomplished:

- The founding of forty-nine convents for her sisters.
- The establishment of training courses for teachers.
- The building of sixty-two schools, including Xavier University.
- Numerous writings.
- Helping to change the attitudes of church people toward the poor and disenfranchised.

- A life of holiness, prayer, and total giving of herself.
- An example of courage, mercy, justice, and compassion.

The Vatican News Service described her life as follows:

In her quiet way, Katharine combined prayerful and total dependence on Divine Providence with determined activism. Her joyous incisiveness attuned to the Holy Spirit, penetrated obstacles and facilitated her advances for social justice. Through the prophetic witness of Katharine Drexel's initiative, the Church in the United States was enabled to become aware of the grave domestic need for an apostolate among Native Americans and Afro-Americans. She did not hesitate to speak out against injustice, taking a public stance when racial discrimination was in evidence.[13]

Katharine Drexel died on March 3, 1955, after living for Jesus and walking in compassion for almost a century.

The Mother of the Holiness Movement— Phoebe Palmer

Phoebe (nee Worrall) Palmer was born in New York City on December 17, 1807. Her father, Henry Worrall, was a devout Methodist who had experienced a radical conversion during the Wesleyan Revival in England before he immigrated to America. He married an American, Dorothea Wade.

Phoebe's parents made sure that they had family worship twice a day in their home. They placed high value on "religious conversion and holy living" for themselves and their children.[14]

When she was only eleven years old, Phoebe wrote this poem on the flyleaf of her Bible:

> This revelation—holy, just, and true
> Though oft I read, it seems forever new;
> While light from heaven upon its pages rest,
> I feel its power, and with it I am blessed.
> Henceforth, I take thee as my future guide,
> Let naught from thee my youthful heart divide.
> And then, if late or early death be mine,
> All will be well, since I, O Lord, am Thine![15]

Throughout her life Phoebe kept the Bible as her guidebook, and the power of the Word motivated her to spread the concept of holiness throughout America in great love and compassion for everyone she met.

Phoebe married a homeopathic physician in 1827. His name was Walter Clarke Palmer, and he, like Phoebe, was an active member of the Methodist Episcopal Church. His parents, Miles and Deborah Clarke Palmer, had helped establish the denomination in New York City.

The young couple shared a commitment to Christ and each other, but their marriage and faith were severely tested by a series of hardships and tragedies, including the deaths of three of their children. At first, Phoebe felt that the deaths of her children were evidence of God's displeasure with her, and she began to question her salvation as she struggled with despair, guilt, and remorse.

This thrust her into a deeper pursuit of God and His ways. After the death of her second son, she wrote, "I will not attempt to describe the pressure of the last crushing trial. Surely I needed it, or it would not have been given. God takes our treasure to heaven, that our hearts may be there also. The Lord had declared himself a jealous God, he will have no other gods before him. After my loved ones were snatched away, I saw that I had concentrated my time and attentions far too exclusively, to the neglect of the religious activities demanded. Though painfully learned, yet I trust the lesson has been fully apprehended. From henceforth, Jesus must and shall have the uppermost seat in my heart."[16]

Phoebe's sister Sarah Lankford began having weekly prayer meetings with Methodist women. Within two years or so, Phoebe assumed leadership of these meetings, which became known as "the Tuesday Meeting for the Promotion of Holiness." Eventually men began to attend these gatherings as well. As word of these meetings spread around the country, a great interest began to develop in what became known as the Holiness Movement.

Phoebe and her husband became itinerant preachers, and they received invitations to speak on holiness—the "deeper work of grace"—from churches, conferences, and camp meetings. Phoebe's work encouraged many other women to start meetings for the promotion of holiness throughout America.

In the autumn of 1857 the Palmers went to Hamilton, Ontario, Canada, to speak at an afternoon prayer meeting. This prayer meeting turned into a ten-day revival in which hundreds of people chose Christ as their Savior.

When they returned to New York, they preached to standing-room-only crowds, and then they traveled to England, where many found faith in Christ. They remained in England for a few years, and it is estimated that more than 25,000 people came to the knowledge of Christ through Phoebe's ministry.

The Palmers believed in a deeper work of grace that would lead to holiness, and this concept was based on John Wesley's idea of Christian perfection, a belief that a Christian can live a life free of serious sin. This "deeper work of grace" was what the Palmers called "entire sanctification."[17]

Without any question, Phoebe Palmer played a prominent role in spreading the concept of Christian holiness throughout America and around the world. She wrote several books on this topic, including *The Way of Holiness*, a foundational book in the Holiness movement. She was very influential in the lives of several women, including Frances Willard, a leading advocate in the Temperance movement, and Catherine Booth, the cofounder of the Salvation Army.

In her book *The Promise of the Father,* Phoebe Palmer took a strong stand for the role of women in Christian ministry. She based this on Acts 5:29, which urges us to obey God rather than men. She said, "It is always right to obey the Holy Spirit's command, and if that is laid upon a woman to preach the gospel, then it is right for her to do so; it is a duty she cannot neglect without falling into condemnation."[18] Her teaching opened the door for many women preachers to respond to God's call in their lives.

Phoebe's holiness was reflected in every aspect of her life, and it impelled her to help found the Five Points Mission in a slum area of New York City in 1850. She also served as a leader in the Methodist Ladies' Home Missionary Society. Her faith had "legs," as it moved in compassion among the dregs of society.

Other influential books by Phoebe Palmer include *Entire Devotion to God* and *Faith and Its Effects,* both of which were published in the 1840s.

When her daughter Eliza was accidentally burned to death as the result of a fire in her nursery, Phoebe wrote these words that prophetically described what her life and ministry truly became:

While pacing the room, crying to God, amid the tumult of grief, my mind was arrested by a gentle whisper, saying, "Your Heavenly Father loves you. He would not permit such a great trial, without intending that some great good proportionate in magnitude and weight should result. He means to teach you some great lesson that might not otherwise be learned."…My darling is in heaven doing an angel service. And now I have resolved that the service, or in other words, the time I would have devoted to her, shall be spent in work for Jesus. And if diligent and self-sacrificing in carrying out my resolve, the death of this child may result in the spiritual life of many.[19]

Phoebe Palmer held true to this commitment until her death on November 2, 1874, and as a result, thousands came to know Christ personally, walking in holiness throughout their lives.

Champion of the Disenfranchised—Hannah More

Hannah More was born at Stapleton, near Bristol, England, in 1745, the youngest of the five daughters of Jacob More, who had been a Presbyterian but became a member of the Church of England. Jacob was a teacher, and his older daughters followed in his footsteps by founding a boarding school at Bristol. Hannah became a pupil in her sisters' school when she was twelve years old and eventually became a teacher there as well.

Hannah began writing for publication when she was still a teenager. Her early works were mostly pastoral plays written for young ladies. She became engaged to William Turner, a wealthy squire who was twenty years older than she, but the couple never married. Even so, William provided Hannah with an annuity that enabled her to become financially independent.

By the mid-1790s, Hannah had become closely involved with the Clapham Sect of evangelical Christians, a group that was very involved in the abolitionist movement. Well-known anti-slavery advocate William Wilberforce and former slave captain John Newton attended this group's meetings as well. She was the most influential female member of the Society for the Effecting the Abolition of the African Slave Trade, and wrote a number of religious tracts, several of which opposed slavery and the slave trade, that eventually led to the formation of the Religious Tracts Society.

Hannah became friends with Wilberforce and other anti-slavery leaders, including John Newton, who wrote "Amazing Grace," and in 1788 she published a poem titled "Slavery." In the late 1780s Hannah and her sister, Martha More, conducted philanthropic work in the Mendip area, a poor coal-mining region. They had set up twelve schools by 1800, and in these schools, reading, the Bible, and Christian teaching were central. They encountered considerable opposition along the way, because many farmers felt that education would become fatal to agriculture.[20] At the same time, the Anglican clergy of the area accused Hannah of having "Methodist tendencies."[21]

Clearly, Hannah blazed a trail for women in her day. She believed in justice for all people and was a pioneer in the abolitionist movement, which eventually brought an end to slavery in Great Britain and the United States. She was also instrumental in the establishment of Sunday schools in the Wrington, England, area, and in these schools poor children were taught reading, religion, and personal hygiene. She chose to get involved in the world instead of living a life of quiet obscurity.

In her life we see a woman who was a great "...example of balance: the hearts of Mary and Martha beating within the same bosom. Hannah More proves that you can be passionate about His presence and at the same time be a servant to fellow man. She earned credibility in two realms, so that both worlds would heed her invitations. If you build it He will come...and they will come to see Him."[22]

As a prolific writer of dramas, poetry, and prose, she became quite wealthy as a result of the publication of her numerous books, plays, poems, and tracts. In fact, she developed a "cottage industry" that enabled her to print millions of religious tracts, which were distributed around the world.

Many of her works were spiritually and ethically influential in the lives of women: *Strictures on Female Education* (1799), *Character of a Young Princess* (1805), *Practical Piety* (1811), *Christian Morals* (1813), *Character of St. Paul* (1815), and *Moral Sketches* (1819). Even though most of her writings have been forgotten now, they were extremely popular and highly marketable during her day, and they had a great impact on women throughout the English-speaking world. She wrote, "Prayer is not eloquence, but earnestness; not the definition of helplessness, but the feeling of it; not figures of speech, but earnestness of soul."[23]

When she died in 1833, Hannah More left the equivalent of three million dollars to charities and religious societies. In one of her poems, she writes about her heavenly home, where she now resides:

> The soul on earth is an immortal guest,
> Compelled to starve at an unreal feast;
> A pilgrim panting for the rest to come;
> An exile, anxious for his native home.[24]

Prison Reformer—Elizabeth Fry

Elizabeth (nee Gurney) Fry was born in Norwich, England, on May 21, 1780. Her father was John Gurney, a successful businessman who was a member of the Society of Friends (Quakers). He was a partner in the Gurney Bank and the owner of a wool-stapling and spinning factory. Elizabeth's mother, Catherine Gurney, was a member of the Society of Friends as well, and she was extensively involved in charity work among the poor. Catherine required her children to spend two hours a day in quiet worship of the Lord.

Elizabeth was twelve when her mother died soon after the birth of her twelfth child. As one of the older daughters, she was required to help in the raising of her younger siblings, which caused Elizabeth to grow up fairly quickly. She became familiar with the writings of Mary Wollstonecraft, who wrote *Vindication of the Rights of Women,* and studied the writings of the abolitionists of her day. At this point in her life, Elizabeth seemed to be heading in a non-religious direction.

However, when she was eighteen years old, Elizabeth heard an American Quaker named William Savery preach in Norwich. She was so impressed by what Savery had to say that she begged her father to invite the preacher to dinner. Her father did so, and after her meeting with Savery, Elizabeth wrote these words: "Today I felt there is a God. I loved the man as if he was almost sent from heaven—we had much serious talk and what he said to me was like a refreshing shower on parched up earth."[25]

This was a dramatic turning point in Elizabeth's life. She wrote, "After we had spent a pleasant evening, my heart began to feel itself silenced before God and without looking at others, I felt myself under the shadow of the wing of

God....After the meeting my heart felt really light and as I walked home by starlight, I looked through nature up to nature's God."[26]

The "showers" from heaven that Elizabeth experienced that night led her to make a momentous decision in her life. From then on she determined to devote her energies to helping needy people. She began to collect used clothing for the poor, she visited the sick, and she opened a Sunday school in her home where she taught poor children to read.

She wrote, "Since my heart was touched...I believe I never have awakened from sleep, in sickness or in health, by day or by night, without my first waking thought being, 'how best I might serve my Lord.'"[27] Clearly, her conversion to Christ went deep, and its repercussions were felt around the world. Soon thereafter she was appointed to the committee that was responsible for running the Society of Friends' school at Acworth.

In the summer of 1799, Elizabeth met Joseph Fry, a Quaker who was the son of a prosperous merchant in Essex. They were married in the summer of the following year, and God blessed the young couple with eight children.

In March 1811, Elizabeth became a preacher for the Society of Friends. A friend, Stephen Grellet, told Elizabeth about the horrific conditions that existed at Newgate Prison, which he had recently visited. He was particularly shocked by the way the women who were incarcerated there were being treated. They had to sleep on the floor without nightclothes or any kind of bedding, and three hundred women were huddled together in only two wards. These prisoners had to cook, wash, and sleep in the same cell.

Elizabeth decided to visit the women of Newgate Prison herself, and she did so on a regular basis thereafter. She took clothing to them, would often read the Bible to them, and started a school and chapel in the prison. As time went on, she established a new system of administration there as well, and this included matrons and monitors who supervised the women.

Meanwhile, Elizabeth continued her duties as a wife and mother, and three more children were born, although she grieved the loss of her five-year-old daughter, Betsy.

Elizabeth and eleven other Quakers founded the Association for the Improvement of the Female Prisoners in Newgate. In her address to the House of Commons, Elizabeth described the conditions of the women in Newgate Prison: "...each with a space of about six feet by two to herself...old and young, hardened offenders with those who had committed only a minor offence or their first crime; the lowest of women with the respectable married women and maid-servants."[28]

Her work influenced major changes in the penal system in Great Britain, which punished prisoners harshly. Richard Huntsman writes:

> For misdemeanours such as causing a nuisance, the culprit would expect physical punishments such as being whipped, branded or put in the stocks. For minor offences, such as stealing a teaspoon or merely begging, one could, before 1775, expect transportation to North America for 7 or 14 years to serve as an indentured labourer or servant. During that period some 40,000 men and women were transported to North America and the West Indies. For what were seen as serious offences ranging from murder, forgery or stealing any object worth over 5 shillings (a week's wage for a maid 'living in'), one would expect to be hanged. Hence the advice that you might as

well be hanged for stealing a sheep as a lamb! In all, over 300 offences attracted the death penalty.[29]

It was these unjust penalties and unfair conditions that caused Elizabeth Fry to get fully involved in prison reform. Between 1818 and 1843, Elizabeth visited prisons throughout the British Isles and the continent of Europe. It was an exhausting and dangerous journey. She would seek the approval of local officials before entering the prisons, and after her visits, she would organize a ladies' association to continue her work in each local prison.

She also became involved as an advocate for women who were sentenced to death. Often she was able to save them from being hanged. Her constant prayer was, "O Lord, may I be directed what to do and what to leave undone."[30]

In 1824, Elizabeth visited Brighton and was shocked by the number of beggars and poor people she encountered there. This led her to form the Brighton District Visiting Society, a group of women who would visit in the homes of the poor and provide them with physical, emotional, and spiritual help and comfort. She campaigned for the homeless in London and tried to improve the care that was given to mental patients in the asylums throughout England. She also worked arduously for the reform of workhouses and hospitals throughout her country.

Nursing care became another one of Elizabeth's concerns. She established a training school for nurses in 1840. Florence Nightingale once wrote to Elizabeth to let her know what a great influence she had been in her life. In 1840, Fry founded the Protestant Sisters of Charity, an organization of nurses who made themselves available to families in need. She often met with Queen Victoria, and the monarch contributed money to her ministry. The queen wrote that she considered Elizabeth Fry to be a "very superior person."[31]

In 1827, Elizabeth published a book, *Observations on the Visiting, Superintendence and Government of Female Prisoners,* in which she showed the need for prison reform and called for greater opportunities for women. She also condemned the death penalty.

After a short illness, Elizabeth Fry died on October 12, 1845. Over a thousand mourners stood in silence as she was buried at the Society of Friends graveyard at Barking. She was a woman of eminent compassion and strong faith who surely believed these words of Paul: "The only thing that counts is faith expressing itself through love" (Gal. 5:6, NIV).

Dear Father in heaven, as did the saints who have lived before me, may I find those who need Your touch of compassion and may I share with them the goodness of Your love. May I find the lost, feed the hungry, speak for the voiceless, and provide shelter for the homeless. Please give me the courage I need to seek out those in the greatest need. In Jesus' name, amen.

Chapter 9

✝

Heidi Baker

BLESSED
ARE THE POOR

(Julia C. Loren)

There are those who talk the talk, and there are others who walk the walk. Heidi Baker is a modern-day apostle of compassion who is living the call—right now.

Heidi is "Mama Ida" to thousands of displaced, abused, and orphaned children who have been raised alongside her own two children, Elisha and Crystalyn. She is truly one who radiates the love, compassion, and joy of the Lord to all she meets. She calls herself a "laid-down lover of God"—one whose life is wholly given over to the Lord, one whose life also inspires others to surrender themselves more completely to the love and service of Jesus. At a Voice of the Apostles conference in 2005, Heidi said, "Fully possessed by the Holy Spirit we become lovers and we do radical things because we know who we are."

In a world that glamorizes the achievements of men, Heidi Baker shuns the spotlight. When she speaks at conferences, those attending tend to see and hear more of Jesus and less of her. Her joy is to fade into the background and let Jesus take over. People weep as the Spirit of God tenderizes their hearts with His compassion for the lost, the broken, and the hurting ones all around the world. Fluent in several languages, she is a gifted communicator with advanced educational degrees.

She also has seen astounding miracles during her thirty years of ministry, especially in Mozambique, where she and her husband, Rolland, and their Iris Ministries team have planted more than seven thousand "bush churches," five Bible schools, and four children's feeding centers since 1990.[1]

Astounding miracles are common to Heidi and Rolland. The blind receive their sight, the deaf hear, and children with AIDS seroconvert to normalcy. Children traumatized by war, severe neglect, and abuse, full of hate, who can barely speak or trust, rapidly respond to their love. Today these same children can be found dancing and ministering with joy. The Bakers have seen God supernaturally multiply food to feed hungry orphans and crowds who gather for meetings. African pastors who have been trained by the Bakers have raised fifty-three people from the dead in Mozambique as of this writing.[2]

The Bakers' lives display the full meaning of Jesus' death and resurrection as they embrace the cross daily—a cross that includes suffering and sacrifice for the sake of releasing healing and reconciling the world to Jesus. It is a cross of compassion and a cross of love.

They spend countless hours soaking in the love of God and interceding for those to whom they minister. Heidi, as a result, has learned that worship is the key to releasing love. And their "intimacy with God provokes confidence that releases faith to stand in God's presence and see Him as big as He is." They live in a place rife with the external evidence of demonic control—war, disease, famine, and corruption. Yet their internal dwelling is "...the place of refuge, a fortress, a secret place of worship and communion. They access a place of blinding, coruscating light. From that place they embark on their mission, to magnify the Lord in the world of men."[3]

Heidi's Calling

Tenacity characterizes this petite blonde, who is originally from Laguna Beach, California. At the age of sixteen, when most Laguna teens were lounging on the beach enjoying the party atmosphere of the era, Heidi was accepted as an American Field Service student. She was sent to a Choctaw Indian reservation in Mississippi, where she was exposed to an environment of poverty that she had never seen before. It was here that she gave her life to Jesus and, after a five-day fast, encountered the Lord in a dramatic way:

> On the night of the fifth day, I expectantly went to the Roark's little Pentecostal church in the country and was drawn to the altar. I knelt down and lifted my arms to the Lord. Suddenly, I felt taken to a new heavenly place. Pastor Roark was preaching, but I couldn't hear his loud, powerful voice at all. God's glory came to me again, wrapping me in a pure and brilliant white light. I was overwhelmed by who He is. I had never felt so loved, and I began to weep. This time He spoke to me audibly. "I am calling you to be a minister and a missionary," He said. "You are to go to Africa, Asia, and England." Again my heart was pounding and racing. I thought I might die.
>
> Then the Lord Jesus spoke to me and told me I would be married to Him. He kissed my hand, and it felt as if warm oil ran down my arm. I was overcome

with love for Him. I knew at that moment that I would go anywhere anytime and say anything for Him. I was ruined for this world by His intense love and mercy in calling me to Himself.[4]

Full of the presence and love of Jesus, Heidi started telling everyone about Him—on the reservation and later at her high school. She talked the local Episcopal priest into letting her start a Christian coffeehouse in the parish hall and ministered every Friday night for several years—praying for the drug addicts, alcoholics, homeless, and demon-possessed people. In the meanwhile, she attended Southern California College (now Vanguard University).

During her last year in college in 1980, she met her husband, Rolland Baker, grandson of well-known missionaries to China who had gained a place in the Church history books for their vital part in launching a revival among Chinese youth in the pre-Maoist years (see H. A. Baker's *Visions Beyond the Veil*).

True to both Rolland's heritage and Heidi's calling, they discerned that they were called together to help bring revival among the poor. Their ministry would be incarnational. They would live like the people, learn the language and the culture from those on the street, suffer with them and earn trust in the process. They married six months later and have since traveled as missionaries to Hong Kong, England, and Mozambique. Their work has extended from Africa into many other countries of the world.

Launched Into Fields of Poverty and War

Their work in Africa began in 1990, when Rolland saw a *Time* magazine article that described the poverty in Mozambique, naming it the poorest country in the world. God knew He needed tenacious and seasoned missionaries and launched them out to start Iris Ministries—working among the Muslims and the poorest of the poor, who were ravished by war, starvation, and disease. The following excerpt best describes their introduction to the mission field:

At the time, the country was involved in a prolonged civil war, and it wasn't until 1995, after a cease-fire was declared between the Renamo (north) and the Frelimo (south), that the Bakers were invited by South African missionaries to go into the war-torn country. They and their friends loaded a few supplies into a red Nissan truck and drove to the border of Mozambique.

To their dismay, the truck sputtered and lost power until, finally, the engine stopped just in front of the border gate between South Africa and Mozambique.

Suddenly, helicopters began flying over them, and people started yelling. The truck in front of them was riddled with bullets from bandits. But as soon as the bandits left and the air cleared, the truck the Bakers were in mysteriously started, so they were able to continue their journey to Maputo, the nation's capital.

The countryside they saw on their way was desolate in the aftermath of the civil war. There were no hospitals or ambulances, but many lay sick or injured as a result of the conflict.

The Bakers struggled to begin a church and an orphanage in a rundown building. In these grim conditions, the Bakers say God displayed His power over poverty one day by multiplying a small amount of chili and rice—originally intended to feed only four people—to such a degree that it was sufficient for not only the Baker family but also 80 orphaned children.[5]

Stopping for One

Stopping for "the one"—the child on the street, the boy scavenging for food in the dump, the girl languishing under forced prostitution—has always been the focus of Heidi's ministry. In the early days after their arrival in Mozambique, they took in dozens of children, many of whom were extremely sick, dying, or angry to the point of violence. Some were healed instantaneously. Others were loved into total emotional, physical, and spiritual health. Others experienced the love of God for a brief time until heaven called them home.

Currently the Bakers and their team care for thousands of orphans living in several children's centers and in the "foster" homes of pastors and widows. Every Iris Ministries pastor, whether he leads a church in a city or in the bush, is encouraged to adopt at least ten orphans. Local widows are summoned to feed and care for the overflow of homeless children who flock to the love offered by the Christians. Many of the children have lost their parents to AIDS in a country where more than 180,000 children are AIDS orphans.

An article in *Charisma* magazine describes the differences in the children before and after Heidi's touch:

> Gitou was an AIDS orphan and a tough street kid when Heidi Baker met him. "He said he was 12, but he looked around 8. His heart was ha7rdened, and he continued telling me off whenever I came near," she recalled. "But I just kept loving and loving Gitou until his heart melted. Now he preaches out on the street and leads many to the Lord."
>
> Constancia was a scared little orphan girl of around 5 who was left on the steps of Iris Ministries' orphanage. "She didn't speak and couldn't communicate,"

Heidi said. "The Lord just told me to chase her…with His love. I'd chase her and hold her until she fell asleep in my arms.

"The same day Constancia was baptized; she began to speak and even asked to lead the choir. She told us then that she'd been mute since seeing her parents brutally murdered right in front of her."[6]

Ever praying about what to do with the overwhelming needs of so many thousands of children and the growing ministry, Heidi received an amazing strategy from the Lord: "The Lord had showed me thousands and thousands of children, and I believe we are called to care for millions of children. At first I was absolutely overwhelmed with that vision, and I thought, 'God how could that ever happen? How could we ever do that, just stopping for the one? I don't know how we could ever, ever do that.' I was praying, crying, fasting and asking God, and He said that He would bring a great revival, and in this revival He would touch the hearts of pastors, and they would become fathers of the fatherless. He said that was His answer for these children. They would be literally cared for by these Mozambican pastors. And then He told me that the widows would cook for them and feed them, that the widows would help farm and that we were to build indigenous buildings made of mud and straw, buildings that fit in with every church. We would see these children cared for in families."[7]

From Struggling Missionary to Apostolic Anointing

Heidi and Rolland labored for years in Africa, and this lifestyle eventually took a toll on Heidi's spirit. Yet her ever-expanding heart of love ached to do more. She tells what happened next:

"Now in Africa we were seeing the sequel to the revival Rolland's grandfather saw among his orphans in China. That was not an isolated outpouring without further fruit. In it Rolland and I saw the heart of God. We saw how He feels about the lost and forgotten. We saw how He delights to use the helpless and hopeless to accomplish His best work. We saw His pleasure in revealing Himself to those humble and poor in spirit enough to appreciate Him. We saw His ability to use simple children to ignite revival. Now we are seeing Him do the same thing in Mozambique. And what He was doing in our children's center fired our appetites all the more for revival.

"We were simply desperate for more of God.

"In January of 1998, Randy Clark was [in Toronto] preaching about the apostolic anointing, laying down our lives and the holy fire of God. He pointed to me and said, 'God is asking, Do you want Mozambique?' I experienced the heavenly fire of God falling on me. I was so hot I literally thought I was going to burn up and die. I remember crying out, 'Lord, I'm dying!' I heard the Lord clearly speak to my heart, 'Good, I want you to be dead!' He wanted me to be completely emptied of self so He could pour even more of His Spirit into my life.

"For seven days I was unable to move. Rolland had to pick me up and carry me. I had to be carried to the washroom, to the hotel and back to the meeting. The weight of His glory was upon me. I felt so heavy that I could not lift my head."[8]

Unable to speak or move for seven days, the presence of God changed Heidi's life. She had never felt so humbled, poor, and vulnerable. Engulfed in the presence of the Lord, she listened as God spoke to her about relinquishing control of her life and the ministry to Him. He spoke of planting hundreds of churches in Mozambique. Where Heidi and Rolland labored for several years with seemingly little fruit, God would burst in with His power and unleash His presence over the region.

"It had taken us seventeen years to plant four churches, and two of them were pretty weak. As I lay there, engulfed in His presence, He spoke to me about hundreds of churches being planted in Mozambique. I remember laughing hysterically, thinking I would have to be two hundred years old before that promise was fulfilled!

"God showed me that I needed to learn to work with the rest of His Body…

"I thought I had been depending on Him to plant churches, when in reality I depended a lot on my own abilities. Naturally, things moved pitifully slowly. It's comical to think we can do God's work for Him. It's all grace. He allows us to participate with Him, and so there is always enough. He showed me how much I needed Him and the body of Christ. He is calling us to complete humility and gentleness. It is never about us; it is always about Him."[9]

After that transforming encounter, everything in Heidi's ministry changed. She returned to Mozambique and began releasing people into ministry, recognizing potential ministers even in young children. She relinquished control and started delegating responsibilities. In return came the apostolic anointing to heal the sick, cast out demons, raise the dead, see blind eyes open and deaf ears hear, and train and launch hundreds of pastors into the largely Muslim fields of Mozambique, where they had labored for years to plant a handful of churches. Now they were shocked to discover the Lord empowering them to plant thousands more in record time.

Keys to Fruitfulness

The Bakers say that one of the keys to becoming a successful ministry lies in relinquishing complete control to God, a concept the Western church needs to learn in order to sow effective ministry throughout the earth. Another key to fruitfulness, the couple says, is intimacy with God. "Revival breaks out when people are desperate for God. When they become intimate with Him and lose sight of themselves, then anything can happen," says Rolland.

One of the most important keys to sustaining successful ministry, however, is tenacious faith to persevere through opposition. Heidi and Rolland Baker articulate the price they pay as they come against the demonic strongholds—a price that includes theft of ministry resources, sickness, malicious lies, and political backlash. They have faced guns and violence. Not one New Creation Power Broker on the mission field today leads an easy life coasting along in a bullet-proof bubble of the Holy Spirit, untouched by human suffering and demonic attack. They need the miraculous power of God every day.

Here is the Bakers' mission-field perspective: "Some who hear us in conferences may come away with the impression that we lead a charmed, tribulation-free life of endless miracles! We do prefer to give Jesus and His glorious power most of the attention in our ministry, but it may encourage you to know that, like Paul, we are jars of clay who glory also in our weakness. When we are weak, then we are strong (2 Cor. 12:10). We do encounter fierce, demonic opposition, and its intensity is almost incomprehensible. This Mozambican province where we live has been a pagan, occult stronghold for centuries, and the evil we encounter shocks us over and over. Our time, energy, funds, and resources are viciously attacked and drained as the devil aims to turn our hearts away from this great revival in which God has graciously placed us.

"Together with Paul, we understand that these things happen that we might not rely on ourselves but on God, who raises the dead (2 Cor. 1:9). We resist the devil by overcoming evil with good, and by resting in Him with all the more faith and childlike joy. We cannot lose while secure in His heart. We have no need to shield ourselves, but we entrust our souls to a faithful Creator in doing what is right (1 Pet. 4:19). The God who has raised at least 53 people from the dead among our churches in Africa will also renew and refresh us with His incomparable power. He will not fail us; we are His workmanship!"[10]

It is their tenacious faith that enabled them to remain in Mozambique long enough to see a breakthrough, not only in church plants, but in increasing miracles, as this 2006 report in *Charisma* magazine reveals:

The miracles are a big part of the Bakers' method for winning Muslims to Jesus. Heidi says they do it "by signs, wonders, and caring for the orphan and the widow. It's love and stopping for the one."

According to her report, however, their target audience is not immediately receptive. "At first the Muslims throw rocks," she says, "but once they see signs and wonders and practical love they can't resist. My ministry team are 8-, 10- and 12-year-olds. Barefoot children in raggedy shirts lay hands on the crippled and they walk."

One day, Heidi took some of these children with her to minister to some synchronistic Muslims (who combine Islam with traditional animistic beliefs) in the city of Pemba.

"They're not a happy bunch," she says. "My kids were ducking rocks, and one hit me low in the back. I jumped up and said, 'Bring me the deaf! Bring me the blind!'"

The team was led through the darkness to an old man who was both lame and blind. He got saved and then said, "I have a headache."

The Bakers' children prayed over him. He was still blind and crippled. Heidi told him, "When you are healed tomorrow, send me a runner." Heidi returned to their meeting place and again asked, "Anybody else blind?" A blind man was brought to her and she said, "I bless him in the name of Jesus."

Heidi says when the blind man screamed, "Ahhhhh! I can see!" the villagers finally stopped throwing rocks.

The next day a runner came up to the car she was sitting in with one of the most influential Muslim men in Pemba and reported, "The blind man can see! He's at his farm working." The man in the car grabbed Heidi's hand and stuck it on his head, tears running down his face. "Pray for me!" he said.

The explosive growth of their ministry is due to the miraculous power that God has released through them in the past decade. The gospel is advancing whole villages at a time as the Holy Spirit's power is poured out, resulting in healing released through compassion and love.

Faith for Healing

Heidi's faith for healing and refreshing has been tested over and over again, and she has persevered to help bring healing to others even as she herself has struggled to receive God's healing.

In 2006, Heidi lay dying from a methicillin-resistant staph infection in a hospital in Johannesburg, South Africa. It was her seventh hospitalization for the infection doctors attributed to her work among the street children. Her two children, away in the United States attending a ministry school, stood vigil in prayer. Rolland cancelled his commitments to remain by her side and sent out urgent requests for corporate prayer. But Heidi had already decided that, like the apostle Paul, although she would love to be with the Lord, it would be better for her to remain in the flesh and continue the work of the ministry. And, characteristically of her tenacious faith, she cried out, "I'm not going out like this!"

The report from *Charisma* magazine summarizes her miraculous recovery from that last life-threatening bout with the infection:

> Heidi checked herself out of the hospital two times. The first time she flew to Pemba, Africa, where hundreds of Mozambicans came to the airport to greet her and sing and dance for her healing. Although she was experiencing incredible pain, she preached to a tent full of people from the Makua and Makonde tribes.
>
> That evening, 55 Makua ran forward to give their lives to Jesus. The Bakers were thrilled with the souls saved, but Heidi's body remained wracked with pain, and following the meeting she flew back to Johannesburg for further treatment.
>
> After returning to the hospital and taking antibiotics for another month, Heidi still had not recovered. The doctors told Heidi there were more advanced drugs in California—her only hope for healing.
>
> Heidi packed her bags and told the medical staff, "I'm going to see a Specialist in Toronto."
>
> She checked herself out of the hospital for the second time and flew to Toronto, to the Toronto Airport

Christian Fellowship, home of what is now known as the Toronto Blessing. Heidi lay on the floor with a pillow, soaking in the presence of God, too sick to get up and participate in worship.

When it was time for her to preach, she felt she had to stand. Weakened and suffering with intense pain, she began her message from Zechariah.

"The fire of God pulsated through my body," Heidi says. "I was literally healed as I preached. There was no pain by the end of the service—it disappeared."

At the end of the meeting, Heidi danced across the platform in thanksgiving to God. Rolland claims tenacity is part of the DNA of a good missionary. "If faith is not exciting to you, don't sign up," he says.

Heidi agrees. "Tenacity is part of the kingdom. King Jesus will win, and we stand on His side."[11]

The Future is Jesus

Rather than burning out (physically and spiritually) on the mission field and giving up, consumed with worry over funds and food shortages, and rather than flickering out in middle age after decades of ministry, Heidi and Rolland are burning ever stronger, completely dependent on God. Heidi has come to know of the love of God more keenly through the suffering orphans they minister to daily, orphans who reflect the face and heart of God.

"It is a privilege beyond price to see the joy and affection of the Holy Spirit poured out like a waterfall on people who have known so much severe hardship, disappointment and bitter loneliness in their lives," Baker wrote in her online ministry report. "From the freezing cold gypsy huts of eastern

Bulgaria to the 115 degree heat of Sudanese refugee camps, from the isolated native Inuits of arctic Canada to the dirt-poor subsistence farmers along the Zambezi River, we see ravenous desire for God among the poor and lowly. Jesus knows their suffering, and He will make it up to them. He will be their God, and they will be His people. He will use them to shame the wise and make the world jealous of their wealth toward Him."

As for how the Lord is using Heidi, she too is shaming the wise and making the world recognize that compassion releases the anointing of Jesus. For a laid-down lover of God, anything is possible. She says:

"I'm so desperate to stay in this place of abandonment. From this place, nothing is impossible. I have only one message—passion and compassion. We're passionate lovers of God, so that we become absolutely nothing. His love fills us. When it's time to stand up, God stands up with us. We focus on His face, never on our ministry, anointing, or numbers.

"All I want to do is love God and care for His people. I find them in the garbage, under trees dying of AIDS. I'm just really simple. Jesus said, 'Look into my eyes,' and everything completely changed. His eyes are filled with love and passion and compassion. Jesus always stops for the dying man, the dying woman and the dying child. That's all I know, passion and compassion. He calls me to love every single person I see every single day.

"Just focus on His face. You will only make it to the end if you can focus on His face. Focus on His beautiful face. You can't feed the poor, you can't go to the street, you can't see anything happen unless you see His face. One glance of His eyes, and we have all it takes to lie down. We're not afraid to die."[12]

Loving People Back to Life

Having led intercessory and equipping teams on site in Mozambique to co-labor with Iris Ministries, I can give you a firsthand report. I agree with John Crowder's statement in his marvelous book, *Miracle Workers, Reformers, and The New Mystics,* "Heidi has no formula for raising the dead except that she literally loves people back to life. She has held the dead bodies of babies and others, weeping over them for hours, until warmth came back into them and they were supernaturally revived."[13] This indeed is compassion in action.

As she globe-trots the nations spreading the fire of the Father's great love, often you can hear Heidi devotionally singing a song that pierces your heart: "I want to be a laid-down lover!" Want to join the song?

> Dear Lord God Almighty, thank You for the strength and courage You have given those who are Your laid-down lovers. Thank You for those who reach out to the poor—one child, one person at a time. Help me to become like those who seek to help and comfort others. I need Your face before me to focus on and to draw power from; I need You to show me the way. In the precious name of Jesus, amen.

Part Three

Living
The Call

This final part of our book is a call to compassion and action to help relieve the horrific conditions of the poor in our world. The Bible says, "Vindicate the weak and fatherless; do justice and maintain the rights of the afflicted and destitute. Rescue the weak and needy; rescue them from the hand of the wicked" (Ps. 82:3–4). This is what the women portrayed in Part Two did, and it is what you and I must do as well.

> Heavenly Father, help us to become a compassionate people. Change our concepts, eradicate our prejudices, demolish our mental strongholds, transform our minds, and give us a strong desire to be merciful and compassionate to all we come in contact with. Let us be agents of change in our world today. In Jesus' name, amen.

Chapter 10

IT'S GOT TO BE PERSONAL

(James W. Goll)

I grew up in a rural area of Missouri, and I have lived in a beautiful country setting in Tennessee with my family. Because of my background of living in rural, agricultural areas, I know something about seed time and harvest. From that vantage point, I realize that there is great power in the hidden seeds that are planted in God's good earth.

Under the direction of my parents, along with my sisters, I helped plant many gardens during the spring of each year. Later, in July and August, I weeded many rows of corn, potatoes, green beans, tomatoes, and many other colorful and leafy vegetables. I often wondered why I had to work so hard in the hot and humid weather, but when fall and winter arrived, I understood and appreciated why I did so. My mom made the best vegetable soup, and to this day, I can still taste its luscious flavor and smell its enticing aroma that filled the entire house.

I learned a great deal from the principle of seedtime and harvest from those garden experiences, and later in life found it to be one of the major guiding biblical principles as well.

Michal Ann also enjoyed the bounty of large gardens when she was growing up. In addition to this, her dad loved using his old cider press to make apple and pear cider. In order to make those delicious natural beverages, however, one first needs fruit. So Michal Ann and the rest of her family would go into the orchards and pick the fruits her father needed to make his favorite recipe. In fact, a Willard family song that is still sung at family gatherings is the "Johnny Appleseed Song." In harmonious unity they sing with all their hearts, giving glory and thanks to God for the harvest He has provided.

Seeds of Compassion

Our job, as believers, is to plant seeds of compassion in a personal way wherever we go, in much the same way that John Chapman ("Johnny Appleseed") planted seeds from apples throughout the United States during the late eighteenth century. We plant the seeds, and God gives the harvest. This is just as true in the spiritual realm as it is in the natural. As we sow seeds of compassion into the lives of others, we look to God to water, cultivate, groom, and prune the emerging seedlings so they will bring forth fruitfulness in due season in the lives of those to whom we minister. There is phenomenal power in the hidden seed.

Sharon Salzberg writes, "Any ordinary favor we do for someone or any compassionate reaching out may seem to be going nowhere at first, but may be planting a seed we can't see right now. Sometimes we need to just do the best we can and then trust in an unfolding we can't design or ordain."[1]

In one of my favorite verses, Paul points out that God will supply the seed for you: "Now He who provides seed for the sower and bread for food will provide and multiply your seed for sowing [that is, your resources] and increase the harvest of your righteousness [which shows itself in active goodness, kindness, and love]" (2 Cor. 9:10). The psalmist David adds for us, "He has dispersed abroad, He has given to the poor; His righteousness endures forever; His horn will be exalted with honor" (Ps. 112:9, NKJV).

If your intention is to know God and serve Him by ministering to others, He will supply your seed to sow. He will make His all-sufficient grace abound toward you, and He will multiply your resources. From His seed fruit will grow the fruit that is called "the fruit of the Spirit" (see Gal. 5:22–23). And there will be a harvest. You can count on that. But remember, the seedlings of love are what will bring a great reward.

Champions of Faith, Hope, and Love

The Holy Spirit is looking for champions in our day. Michal Ann and I have written about many of these valiant heroes in the Women on the Frontlines series, in which the book you are now reading is the third volume. There are many champions, both great and small, who have made it into "God's Hall of Heroes." Some of these good people we may never meet or know until we see them in heaven, but others, such as Rolland and Heidi Baker of Iris Ministries, are modern-day trailblazers and pacesetters from whom each of us can learn a great deal.

All too often we focus on the gigantic exploits that are done by great people of faith, but we must never forget that little acts of love and kindness often precede public displays of power. Each of us must go through a hidden preparation period in which we learn how to walk in compassion and, as in any process, we have to take "baby steps" at first. This is the seed-planting stage.

Michal Ann and I have had the pleasure of knowing Mahesh and Bonnie Chavda for many years. As many already know, it was the healing prayers of Mahesh that paved the way for the Lord to bless us with our four beautiful children. I have often said, "Mahesh is not a show horse; he is a work horse!"

In the earlier days of my ministry, I had the privilege of doing some behind-the-scenes work for Mahesh's meetings as he traveled around the United States and internationally. I remember getting drinks for him, serving as a "catcher," fetching his tennis shoes so his tired feet could be more comfortable after praying with people until 2:00 A.M., and enjoying the fun of fellowship with him.

What always impressed me the most, as I observed and learned from Mahesh, was how he always took time for each individual. He never seemed to be in a rush; he ministered to each person as though every single individual was the most important person in the meetings. The Bakers and the Chavdas are both modern-day examples of the power of taking time for the one—always making it personal. The following is a story that was taken from Mahesh's first book, *Only Love Can Make a Miracle*. It shows how his heart of compassion and his ministry began to bloom.

Only Love Can Make a Miracle

"The Lord gave me an overwhelming love for children. It was hard to explain. It was as though the Lord broke off a little piece of His heart and placed it inside me. I loved those children as though they were my own.

"I used to work a nine-hour shift in Lily, usually with the ambulatory children, those who were able to get around on their own. When I was off duty, I would go to the non-ambulatory wards just to be with the children there. I had such a love for them. The thought of them having to spend the rest of their lives in those cribs almost broke my heart.

"I knew that God loved them, too, and that he wanted to channel that love through me. I didn't really know what to do with them or even how to pray for them. I used to just hold them and pray quietly in the Spirit. Often I would sit in a rocking chair with one of them for hours, just praying and singing in tongues.

"One little girl especially touched my heart. Her name was Laura. Laura's mother had been using hard drugs during pregnancy, and she had been born blind and severely retarded. I used to rotate through the different non-ambulatory wards on my after-hours visits, but in time I began to gravitate more and more to little Laura. She was so precious to me.

"One day I had occasion to go into Laura's ward during the day. It had been several weeks since I had started holding her and praying with her. As I approached her crib, she turned toward me and stretched out her hands to welcome me! There were a number of staff members nearby. They were amazed. They kept saying to each other, 'Did you see that?' Laura had never shown any outward response to anyone before, not even to being touched. Now she was responding to me from across the room. Could it be that she was gaining her sight? Could it be that the Lord was healing her through my prayers?

"Not long after this, I had a similar experience with a little boy who had been born with a terrible birth defect. His spine was deformed so that he was unable to sit up. Again, after I had been praying with him over a period of several weeks, he suddenly became able to sit up. His back was healed!

"As far as I can recall, I never once specifically prayed that these children be healed. I had prayed that way for my mother because I felt the Lord had told me to. Other than that, prayer for healing was not something I was accustomed to doing.

"When I was with the children, I would simply hold them and pray that the Lord would somehow enable them to experience His love through me. I was as surprised as anyone when they started getting better.

"I was learning many lessons in my school of the Spirit. Now I was learning that the power of God was to be found in the love of God. When the Lord sent me to the State School, he did not say, 'I am sending you as my ambassador of power or of miracles.' He said, 'I am sending you as my ambassador of love.' That was the way I saw myself and that was the way I prayed for the children: that the Lord would make His love real to them. The healings came almost as a by-product. I learned that only love can make a miracle."[2]

Any of us can be an ambassador of love for the Father. His love is powerful; it truly is the stuff of which miracles are made.

Revival of Kindness

The world needs a revival of kindness today. Imagine what would happen if God's people began to use their innate creativity to develop ways to show kindness to others. Simple acts of kindness, stemming from the love of God, would effect major changes in people's lives.

Early one morning I was awakened by the voice of the Holy Spirit speaking to me. The dove of God seemed to be gently whispering secrets to me. In the midst of hearing of coming moves of His manifested presence with signs and wonders and displays of great power, what struck me the most that morning was one simple phrase: "I will have a revival of kindness."

I wrote everything down in a journal by my bedside, and later I shared with Michal Ann about it. That one line went deep within her very being: "I will have a revival of kindness." Perhaps this experience was one of those seeds that put language to what was already growing in Michal Ann's heart, so that eventually she would launch a new ministry called Compassion Acts.

I wonder what our society would really look like if instead of our hurried, dog-eat-dog, frantic pace, we actually took time to pause, breathe, and act a little more like Jesus?

Random Acts of Kindness

I wonder what a revival of kindness looks like. We know of some of the characteristics of power evangelism and crusade evangelism by reading and observing the great revivals of the past. But it seems to me that for a genuine revival of kindness to come to pass, it has to be personal.

In fact, I believe the Holy Spirit wants us to have some fun in the process. Why not try some "random acts of kindness" as seeds to sow? For example:

- Give someone a word of encouragement.
- When in the drive-through line of a fast-food restaurant, pay for the meals that were ordered by the people behind you.
- Take time to be a good listener to someone.
- Get trained and participate in healing rooms or prayer rooms in your area.

- Distribute Bibles and Christian books to people you encounter in your day-to-day activities.
- Randomly give out worship CDs to people in a mall.
- Surrender your place in line to someone who seems to be in a hurry, whether in a supermarket, a bank, or elsewhere.
- Participate in an outreach at a public venue.
- Ask others if you could pray for them and invite the Holy Spirit's presence to come so that God's glory will be revealed.
- Give an unusually good tip to a server in a restaurant and leave them a note telling them that God cares.
- Take bags of groceries to a poor family and leave a note that says, "From the Man Upstairs who sees and cares."
- Invite international college students to your home over the holidays.
- Send cards of encouragement and comfort to those who are alone.
- Invite people to attend church or a time of fellowship with you.
- Tell people in practical ways about the love of Jesus.

All of these "random acts" of kindness are seeds of compassion that will truly make a difference in the lives of others in personal, practical, and tangible ways.

True Compassion Is Always Personal

Compassion is always personal. It costs you something and it releases something. In Webster's *New Collegiate Dictionary*, we read that compassion is "a sympathetic consciousness of others' distress together with a desire to alleviate it." It is more than just a feeling; it is also an action. Compassion gives you insight into another's need, and it enables you to understand their hurts, pain, and heartache.

God will reveal to you what needs to be done to help alleviate another's situation.

Vine's Expository Dictionary of New Testament Words provides us with many additional insights related to compassion by showing us the Greek verbs that are associated with it:

Oikteiro—to have pity, a feeling of distress through the ills of others. This verb is used to describe the compassion of God, which is one of His central attributes. As you can see, God's compassion is always personal and it is directed to individuals in need.

Splanchnizomai—to be moved as within one's inwards; to be moved with compassion, and to yearn with compassion. This is the verb that is frequently used to describe the way Jesus was moved with compassion toward the multitudes and toward individuals.

Do you remember the story of the widow of Nain? Her only son had died. When Jesus saw her, "...He had compassion on her and said to her, 'Do not weep.'" (Luke 7:13, NKJV). The Lord saw the funeral procession for the young man, and He was moved with compassion for the widow who was experiencing a painful sense of loss. Notice the progression here: first He saw, then He was moved with compassion. But it didn't stop there. It went beyond the feeling level and became an act.

Jesus' primary concern in this example did not appear to be the eternal state of the young man; rather, He was concerned about the mother and what she was going through.

He felt compassion for her. Not only did He tell her, "Don't weep," but He also took positive steps to rectify the situation. The Bible says, "And He came up and touched the bier [on which the body rested], and the pallbearers stood still. And He said, 'Young man, I say to you, arise [from death]!'" (Luke 7:14).

Jesus saw. Jesus felt compassion. Jesus spoke words of comfort. Then Jesus moved forward with a touch and a command. The result was: "The man who was dead sat up and began to speak. And Jesus gave him back to his mother" (Luke 7:15).

First we have to perceive (see) the need. Then we speak words of encouragement and comfort, which may often lead us to communicate love and warmth through a touch or an embrace. Next, we take action by doing what we can to provide practical help and assistance to the person in need. One thing we can always do is to pray for him or her, and, as Tennyson said, "More things are wrought by prayer than this world dreams of."

An Eruption of Mercy

Deep within His spirit, Jesus is always in tune with the Father. His intimacy with His Father propelled Him to go out among the people and to be sensitive to their needs. In other words, He looked outside Himself and He saw what others needed. We can do the same, but first we must spend time alone with God in the secret place of the Most High. That is time well-spent, for it empowers us to go forth in love and compassion. A deep yearning arises as we spend time with the Father, and this yearning is focused on helping others.

In his book *Authority to Heal,* Ken Blue tells us that

Jesus' compassion for people was not merely an expression of His will, but rather an eruption from deep within His being.[3] This volcanic image shows us how compassion should work in each of our lives, as an eruption of sympathy, empathy, and mercy flowing out to others like lava from a crater. God's mercies are everlasting, and they are constantly flowing from His throne—a throne that is established on the foundation of righteousness and mercy.

Have you ever noticed that when you get emotional about something, you do something in response to your emotions? When your emotions are stirred up, you take action. You may weep, jump up and down, write a letter, or head in a certain direction with a specific goal in mind. It is the same with God. He gets emotional over us, and it stirs Him to take action on our behalf.

Some things stick with you. I remember so very well many of the journeys I have taken as an intercessory missionary praying "on site with insight." Walking in the Cité Soleil, Port-au-Prince, in impoverished Haiti…how can I forget? The sights, the sounds, and yes, the smells…

As I walked through the areas where little boys wore no clothes, where there were no flushing toilets or anything close to it for that matter, my heart broke. I walked in areas that were not safe according to World Health Organization standards. But God propelled my feet to walk among the poor, praying, caring…and sowing seeds of kindness. I wept as I walked among these precious people. I had a "compassion eruption" that motivated me to go back and forth numerous times from the United States to Haiti, hoping, praying, and longing to make a difference somehow.

Do you want to walk where Jesus did? Then watch out. If you express that desire before God, He might just take you into some really strange and wonderful places. Could it be that the farther we go on our journey with God, the more He wants us to be like Him? Do you want to be like Him? Do you want to follow in the footsteps of the Lord? Do you want His image to be formed in you?

If your answer to these questions is yes, then you must let the necessary ingredient of compassion fill your heart and motivate you to get on the front lines of service for your Lord. God is full of compassion, and His eruptions of love and mercy are yearning to be activated in our lives.

Sweeter Than Honey

Many people do not understand the nature of God—that He is full of mercy and compassion. If we truly understood this, wouldn't it change everything about us? Wouldn't it impel us to get compassionately involved with meeting others' needs, as Jesus was? Jesus certainly understood what is in the Father's heart, and because He does, He was willing and able to go to the cross for us.

As I shared in chapter 2, John Wimber was given a spiritual vision about God's mercy once while driving his car in southern California:

"Suddenly in my mind's eye there appeared to be a cloud bank superimposed across the sky....Then I realized it was not a cloud bank, it was a honeycomb with honey dripping out onto people below. The people were in a variety of postures. Some were reverent; they were weeping and holding their hands out to catch the honey and taste it, even inviting others to take some of their honey. Others acted irritated, wiping the honey off, and complaining about the mess. I was awestruck. Not knowing what to think, I prayed, 'Lord, what is it?'

"He said, 'It's My mercy, John. For some people it's a

blessing, but to others it's a hindrance. There is plenty for everyone. The problem isn't on my end, John. It's down there.'

"What God showed me...was that he is much greater than I ever imagined him to be, and with only the smallest act of faith I could experience his compassion and mercy.

"I also realized that God's mercy is constantly falling on us, because everything that He does is related to what He is: the Father of compassion....Psalm 145:9 says, 'The Lord is good to all; he has compassion on all he has made.'

"...But too often I did not see God in the fullness of his mercy and grace. I trusted him to lead me, but I did not trust him to provide for me; I had faith to receive forgiveness of sins and salvation, but I had no faith for divine healing. I never realized God's mercy was as readily and abundantly available to me as the honey was available to all under the honeycomb.

"...In the vision, some people rejoiced, freely received, and freely gave away. The more they gave away, the more they received. 'There is plenty for everyone,' the Lord said. 'Don't ever beg me for healing again.'

"But others, full of unbelief and skepticism, could not receive the grace, blessings, and gifts of God. They could not see that God's mercy and healing are greater than their understanding of how he works."[4]

Want to Make a Difference?

Do you want to make a difference in the world? Then be different from others by walking in compassion wherever you are. Plant seeds of mercy in soil of desperate people's lives. People will see the difference, and they will want to have what you have. Not only that, but they will receive what they need through the grace on your life.

But compassion always has to be personal. It needs to flow from your heart to the person in front of you. As the writer of one the shortest books in the Bible states, "And on some have compassion, making a distinction" (Jude 1:22, NKJV).

We need a revelation of what compassion really is and what it entails. The God of all compassion and comfort wants to be compassionate in and through you. He lives within you, so let Him and His miracle-working love and compassion flow forth from you and propel you, along with others, into action.

> Jesus, be big in me! Let Your emotions within me be stirred up. By Your grace, I choose to sow seeds of Your radical transforming love and mercy into the lives of others. I volunteer freely to be a part of Your compassionate army walking throughout the nations to bring a revival of kindness. I want to make a difference. Here I am—use me! Amen.

Chapter 11

━━━┿━━━

COMPASSION ACTS

(Michal Ann Goll)

We have journeyed through Scripture, studying God's heart for justice, righteousness, and mercy. We have looked, up close and personal, at the lives of some amazing women and their impact on the world. Before we go any farther, though, we are going to rest. Rest is very important, especially in regard to this call to compassion.

As we open our hearts to feel God's heart, we may feel pressure to "do" something. Where is this pressure coming from? Is it direction from God, or are we beginning to see legitimate needs but moving out of our mental or "soulish" strength rather than out of our spirit? Ah, this is very important! Take time right now to stop and rest. Let your mind and heart center on His presence and worship Him for just a few minutes.

Compassion ministry, or whatever you want to call it, can be draining and exhausting. But it doesn't have to be. It depends on your motivation and your approach. It should not drive you, but rather, God's heart should lead you. Do you see the difference?

Mary and Martha

Do you remember the story about Mary and Martha? I used to think only that "Mary chose the better part," and that Martha was reprimanded. We need to look at the Scripture again.

Martha, dear Martha! She was the one who received Jesus and welcomed Him into her house. Now, she did become distracted with much serving, and that was the point that Jesus spoke tenderly to her, redirecting her heart to "the better part," to worship Him (see Luke 10:40). But I believe He was wooing her, drawing her to Himself, not correcting or belittling her. She had compared her serving and cooking to Mary's "sitting." What a common error that is—a lesson we are still trying to learn.

Yet when Lazarus was sick (see John 11), the sisters sent word to Jesus. By the time He came, Lazarus had been in the tomb for four days. "When Martha heard that Jesus was coming, she went out to meet him, but Mary stayed at home. 'Lord,' Martha said to Jesus, 'if you had been here, my brother would not have died. But I know that even now God will give you whatever you ask'" (John 11:20–22, NIV).

Do you see a pattern here? Not only was it Martha who welcomed Jesus into their house, but when her brother died, she was the one who met Him and asked for her brother's life to be restored. We need Martha. It doesn't have to be, "Are you a Mary or a Martha?" The point is, God wants us to be both. There is no place for comparison in the kingdom of God, and we don't have to choose between either living a life of prayer and devotion, or serving; we are to choose both. It's time for Mary and Martha to come together. After all, they were sisters and they did live in the same house. So should we.

Bowels of Compassion

The bowels are part of the intestinal tract, and though we don't like to talk about that part of the body, we do see an enlightening analogy here. In earlier times the bowels were considered to be the seat of pity, tenderness, and courage. Look at the language of the King James Version: "But whoso hath this world's good, and seeth his brother have need, and shutteth up his bowels of compassion from him, how dwelleth the love of God in him?" (1 John 3:17, KJV).

The bowels are the deepest parts of our bodies, the last stop within our digestive tracts. The food we eat goes through many different processes as it is absorbed by the digestive system, but where we receive the greatest nutrition from our food is as it passes through the bowels.

Similarly, we drink the pure milk of the Word of God (see 1 Pet. 2:2) and we begin to digest its truths, that we might grow. However, we have to get it past our minds. We need to let it find its way into our hearts. It needs to go through every part of our "digestive" process, and if we stop short of the "bowels of compassion," we have missed the greatest release of spiritual nourishment and enrichment. If we listen, take notes, and recite spiritual truth, but never act on it or apply it, all that has happened is that just our brains got bigger and not our hearts.

Paul writes, "Put on therefore, as the elect of God, holy and beloved, bowels of mercies, kindness, humbleness of mind, meekness, longsuffering" (Col. 3:12, KJV). We must *put on* compassion and kindness. This is a decision we must make if we want to follow God's ways. It's a commitment we make to God.

I've had people come up to me at conferences and different gatherings, asking me to pray for them to receive an impartation for compassion. I've thought about this a lot, and I've come to the conclusion that I don't think that is possible. Just as our bodies process the food that causes the bowels to act, so should our spirits, as we process the love of God and His Word, bring our "bowels of compassion" to act. You can't eat food in the physical and not have the process that brings elimination; you can't have one without the other. Compassion acts.

I've been concerned not only about the condition of my own heart, but also the heart of the Church. If we're having a difficult time getting this individually, then how can the kingdom of God advance corporately? The answer is obvious—we can't.

Charles Spurgeon wrote this about compassion: "It is expressive of the deepest emotion; a striving of the bowels—a yearning of the innermost nature with pity....When our Savior looked upon certain sights, those who watched Him closely perceived that His internal agitation was very great, His emotions were very deep, and then His face betrayed it, His eyes gushed like founts with tears, and you saw that His big heart was ready to burst with pity for the sorrow upon which His eyes were gazing. His whole nature was agitated with commiseration for the sufferers before Him."[1]

Jesus Christ is a compassionate Friend to precious souls; His bowels yearn in mercy and pity for those in need. It was this mercy that brought Him from heaven to earth, and it was this mercy that took Him to the cross. His compassion brought Him to action—even dying on the cross for our sins, that we would be forgiven and have fellowship with the Father. His compassion brought action.

Jesus loves you. God the Father loves you. To use a phrase from Graham Cooke, "You can't make Him love you any more, and you can't make Him love you any less." He loves you without reservation, just as you are, right now! That's who He is and what He does. That is the focus of His compassion. He longs and groans for His house to be full, for His table to be full, and it won't be full unless you are there. He desires to draw you to Himself today, and to never be separated from you ever again. He has done it all for you and me.

All you have to do is say yes to Jesus. If you've never said yes to Him before, or maybe He's tugging on your heart in a fresh way, just talk with Him now. Tell him you love Him, you believe in Him, and you want to walk with Him. He will hear you and will answer your prayers.

Paul writes, "Therefore, I urge you, brothers and sisters, in view of God's mercy, to offer your bodies as a living sacrifice, holy and pleasing to God—this is your true and proper worship" (Rom. 12:1, NIV).

This is what is needed today: a decisive dedication of our lives as living sacrifices to God. What better offering can we give to God, in light of all His mercies to us?

The World We Live In

The world is desperate for help. According to recent studies, 75 percent of the world's population lives in poverty. Most of these people live in Third World, or developing, countries. The average annual gross income for individual workers in Western countries is $27,000. Contrast that with the rest of the world, where the average annual gross income is between $450.00 and $2,500.00 per person.[2] What a difference!

Approximately 50 percent of the world's population is female. Women suffer more from poverty than men. Forty percent of the world's population consists of children. They are the ones who suffer more than all others. In fact, over one billion children are at risk today, and many have become victims of extreme poverty, homelessness, the loss of their parents, child labor, abuse, slavery, sexual exploitation, AIDS and other illnesses, and the effects of war and religious persecution.[3]

In certain parts of the world, orphaned children are conscripted into armies, where they suffer sexual, mental, and physical abuse. They are forced to carry guns and trained to kill. At times, the governments involved are willing to "sell off" numbers of these children to ease their financial situations. Finances are needed today for these purposes. I know of dear, precious saints who are working behind the lines to rescue these children, give them hope for their destiny, and restore self-respect and esteem.

Sometimes it can be quite easy to read the words but not engage our hearts in the reality of what they mean. If those children were *our* children, or those people *our* family, don't you think our attitude would be different? I know mine would. That is what the Lord wants to do—to enlarge our hearts to such a degree that "they" become "our family." They are His kids, the love of His heart, and we just don't seem to get it or care. When will we get it? When will we do something about these needs? If there ever was a time for compassion in our world, it is today!

The Deborah Company

There is a need for the Deborah anointing today. (See Judges 5:7 regarding Deborah, "a mother in Israel.") The Israelites were faced with a complete disruption of the entire region. There was no protection for the people. No laws were enforced. The people couldn't even travel on the roads; they had to sneak along hidden pathways because the Philistine army was all about, raiding, killing, plundering their crops and their homes. Then Deborah arose.

The name Deborah means "bee." Like a bee, Deborah was a very industrious woman. She judged Israel, but was particularly devoted to the reestablishment of true biblical worship in the temple. It is said that she spent time making the wicks for the candles that would be used in the temple. How appropriate this is when you realize that the word "Lappidoth," mentioned in Judges 4:4, it is a Hebrew term that deals with light or illumination. Different translations give various meanings to this word. Deborah was either married to a man named Lapidoth, or she came from a region with that name. We see that Deborah, who served as a prophetess and judge in ancient Israel, was a bearer of great light, illumination, and wisdom.

Deborah was a very courageous woman who was not afraid to take risks (see Judg. 4). While she was sitting under her palm tree, a symbol of authority from which she judged, in the hill country of Ephraim, the Israelites came up to her, bringing their grievances concerning the onslaughts from the army of Jabin, the King of Canaan. Then she called for Barak, an army general, and told him to go forth into battle and that God would give him victory over Sisera, the general who was commanding the Philistine army.

Barak responded to her prophecy by saying that he would go to the River Kishon, where the battle would take place, but he would do so only if she would agree to go with him. Deborah said, "I will surely go with you; nevertheless there will be no glory for you in the journey you are taking, for the Lord will sell Sisera into the hand of a woman" (Judg. 4:9, NKJV).

What had Barak seen in Deborah's life that caused him to want her to go into warfare with him? What qualities did she possess that made him feel strengthened in her presence? Why would he ask a woman to take part in the battle with him?

I believe it's because he saw her as a woman of illumination, someone who walked in the light and glory of God. She was a wise, industrious, and brave woman who knew God. Therefore, I believe Barak was saying in effect, "I'm not going to go into battle unless you go with me, unless I have the illumination and presence of God with me."

Deborah had divine illumination and she had the presence of the Lord. Barak, also a prophet, had the administrative ability to raise an army and go out into the field and do the work. Neither one could do without the other, and neither one cared who received the glory. They just wanted to defeat the enemy and to give all the glory to God. And that's what happened (see Judg. 4:22–23). Commerce was restored, villages and families were restored, law and order was restored. When the government of God is set in place, it displaces all other governments.

I believe there is a new release of the Deborah anointing, but this time around it's not given to just one person; it's for a whole company of women who want to see the illumination of God and His kingdom established, and are willing to become breakers in the Spirit—to break it open!

In a similar vein, I believe there is a whole company of Baraks, who don't care if the glory goes to men or women; they just want God to show up—that's all that matters. They are trustworthy and know how to wage war, and how to win.

War Generals

What we're talking about here is the body of Christ coming into formation, becoming connected. In order for us to truly be effective in this battle for compassion, there has to be order, good supply lines, and good communication. I believe the Lord wants to release a whole army of compassionate warriors, and if there is to be a whole army, then there certainly has to be commanders overseeing, directing, and caring for the troops. We need to assemble ourselves together, and gather around those who are farther down the road than we are—ones who are filled with courage, vision, and passion for God. These are men and women who are committed to defending the gospel. They are not afraid of warfare, and they are eager to engage in all necessary battles and are willing to fight.

God wants generals, or breakers, who know His heart. Unlike the world's concept of what a general looks like, God's generals are ones who know authority, yes; but they follow the example of their Master and Savior. They live their lives carrying a towel, ready to love and to serve. They know the meaning of the phrase "lower still." They understand that the authority they carry comes from the greatest servant of all, Jesus.

He calls us to "fight the good fight of faith" (1 Tim. 6:12). With His help we will rise up as the army of God, replete with generals, majors, sergeants, corporals, and privates. We will be "more than conquerors" (Rom. 8:37), carrying our swords, our shields—and our towels.

I hear the sound of horses' hooves pounding the ground and the sounds of victory filling the air. The battle is the Lord's and through Him we will be victorious!

The Innkeeper Anointing

This battle has many fronts. There are some in particular that I feel the Lord is highlighting and sounding a fresh prophetic call. I believe He is releasing specific anointings to accomplish these assignments.

One of them is what I like to call "the Innkeeper anointing." Most of us are familiar with the parable of the Good Samaritan (see Luke 10:30–35). In this story we learn that a certain man had been robbed, stripped, wounded, and left to die. He was slighted by those who should have been his friends and helpers, including a priest who should have known better and a Levite who was supposed to show tenderness and compassion to those in need. When the Levite saw this man, he went over and took a close look at him, then crossed to the other side of the street when he saw the condition he was in. In other words, the Levite got as far away from him as he could.

Another man, a Samaritan, came along, and when he saw the injured man, he had compassion on him. Using his own linen, which he probably tore from his own clothing, he bound up the man's wounds. He poured oil and wine into the man's wounds and then put him on his own donkey. He took him to an inn, put him to bed, and paid the innkeeper for his accommodations.

Previously, I've focused on the Samaritan in this Scripture passage. While the Samaritan anointing is desperately needed and covers a wide range of compassionate acts, I want to acknowledge the innkeeper. He is barely mentioned, but he is also important. We need to have those who will go out into the streets and find the wounded ones, but there has to be some place to bring them in, for full restitution. The innkeeper already has his placement established, rooms available and ready, at a moment's notice. His would be like an extended-care ministry. It may be in the form of recovery facilities, or it could be families who will open up their homes.

This ministry is very practical, and could be very personal. Do you have an extra bedroom the Lord could use?

Are you open for a "Samaritan" to come into your life and drop into your lap someone who needs help? This is one of the anointings that God is releasing among His people today. God wants us to provide for all those who are lying alongside the road in a state of hopelessness, despair, and great need. You don't know how much you have to offer until you see how deep the needs of these people are.

Creative Compassion

We need to ask for answers to questions the world has yet to ask. We need to look into the future, and ask the Lord for creative solutions and inventions. We need to look at ways to create entrepreneurial businesses to create jobs for those in low-income areas, and help boost economies. We need to ask for houses, and look for ones that can be salvaged, repaired, and used for places of recovery or rescue.

How about a marriage of compassion with the prophetic? How about building relationships with our police, finding out the needs of our cities, and developing prophetic intercessory teams who will pray and ask for specific answers? We need to see what we can do to rescue and create a net to catch the women and children who have been trapped in sex-trade businesses and prostitution, and who are looking for a way out.

We need to develop water-filtration systems that are inexpensive and easy to set up in Third World countries. We need to develop supply lines so ministries learn to work together and serve each other. We need to cross over boundary lines of denominations and affiliations, reaching into areas that need help. We need to move forward in kingdom understandings and applications, building relationally—in love.

We need to care for the poor and needy, not only within

our own regions but internationally as well. Africa is dying right now. Our help is needed right now. They need simple things—beans and rice—by the trailer loads. Whole families are being lost. Here in the United States, most major cities are full of kids who have run away from home; they are living on the streets and using drugs. These are our kids—these are our people. Jesus, open our eyes and hearts!

Preparing Our Fields

Being raised in rural Missouri from birth until James and I were married, I have a great appreciation for the biblical language regarding nature and agriculture. I spent many, many hours in the hot sun with an ever-aching back and sunburned arms, weeding our huge vegetable garden, harvesting those vegetables and preparing and storing them. We kept the kitchen stove running for days at a time, canning beans, tomatoes, and various fruits. We processed countless chickens, cutting them up and freezing them. We processed cherries, peaches, apples, pears, raspberries, and plums.

We spent whole days at my grandmother's house fighting our way through endless blackberry thickets, creating tunnels through the tangled maze of thorny canes, and coming home with tubs and tubs full to put in the freezer. I've worked out in the hayfields with my brothers, running the tractor so they could pick up the bales and stack them on the wagon. That hay was necessary for our cattle to make it through the winter. I've known the necessity and value of tending plants, tending gardens and fields. And God says:

"When you reap the harvest of your land, do not reap to the very edges of your field or gather the gleanings of your harvest. Do not go over your vineyard a second time or pick up the grapes that have fallen. Leave them for the poor and the foreigner. I am the Lord your God." (Lev. 19:9–10, NIV)

I believe the Lord is issuing a challenge to us, for we all have "fields" that we are laboring in, fields the Lord has given to us. It's in these fields that we must plant the seeds that will bring forth a bountiful harvest. Everyone has a sphere of influence; it may be your workplace, it may be your home, it may be the school you attend, it may be other people who share your ethnic background or the geographical region where you live.

We must prepare our fields in such a way that we allow the poor and the strangers to benefit from the harvest. The times in which we live make this a very urgent matter, for we see a great increase in natural disasters, terrorism, war, and disease around the globe.

Plant good seed in your field, and be sure to plant what God tells you to plant. While you do so, make certain that you leave some fruit in your field so the poor can reap some from your harvest too.

Rest and Rejoice

The seventh year was meant to be a year of rest and rejoicing. The Bible says, "but the seventh year you shall let it rest and lie uncultivated, so that the poor among your people may eat [what the land grows naturally]; whatever they leave the animals of the field may eat. You shall do the same with your vineyard and olive grove" (Ex. 23:11).

As we get to know the heart of God, we need to get our lives in line with His calendar. The seventh year represents perfection and completion, a fulfillment of the will of God, which demands that the land should lie fallow so the poor can reap a benefit, and so the land can rest. The seventh year was a year of breakthrough and blessing both for the land-owners and the poor. Everyone shared in the good things God had provided for them.

In the book of Esther we read: "...as the days on which the Jews had rest from their enemies, as the month which was turned from sorrow to joy for them, and from mourning to a holiday; that they should make them days of feasting and joy, of sending presents to one another and gifts to the poor" (Est. 9:22, NKJV). We need to enlarge our hearts to include the poor as part of our times of celebration. When deliverance, in whatever form it may take, comes to your house—remember the poor. Let your deliverance spill over to those who are still waiting for their own deliverance to be released.

Time is an intriguing element. We have a past, and we speak of a future. But where both become a reality is *right now*. In reality, now is all that we have. We can do nothing about our past, but if we act now, we can establish what will become our past. We can talk about the future, but the problem is, the future is always ahead of us; we can never live in the future.

We must live in the now. If we try to live in the future, we're always dreaming and never realizing. We need to take our dreams and make practical steps today to see them come to pass. We need to move out of any remorse over past mistakes or missed opportunities, and make a decision to get up and act now.

The Poor Man's Watch

When preparing to go on my first trip to Mozambique to serve Iris Ministries with Rolland and Heidi Baker, I bought a simple plastic watch. It was very cheap, but it actually had more bells and whistles than my nicer watch, and was a great tool for the trip. When I got home, I unpacked my clothes, developed my pictures, gave out gifts to my loved ones, and tried to get my life in order again. There was my nicer watch on my nightstand, waiting for me to take it up again, but something inside me didn't want to put it back on. Days went by, weeks went by, and I just couldn't take this simple cheap little watch off my wrist.

I went to the Lord, asking Him what was going on. Didn't I want to go forward? Was I holding onto something I needed to release? Finally one day my friend, the precious Holy Spirit, spoke to me. He said, "You are on the poor man's watch." This word went through my heart like an arrow. I knew it to be true. There was no taking it off; there was no getting my life back in order. In actuality, my life was getting in God's order.

God has a poor man's watch that is perfect for each one of us. It is not a gift; it's part of the kingdom of God. If we want to experience His kingdom, we have to wear the watch.

Looking for Jesus

I'm looking for Jesus; I'm waiting for Jesus. But could it be that Jesus is waiting for me? Could it be that as I engage my heart to not only hear the Word of God, but to live the Word to those who do not know Him, Jesus just might come to me? That sounds like the kingdom of God coming on the earth. I want to be a part of establishing God's kingdom, and raising up a whole army of like-hearted loving warriors who have embraced the call to compassion. He is waiting for you. Will you enlist in this army? I pray that your answer is yes, and that you are stirred to action—because compassion acts.

Dear Lord Jesus, I come to You this day, volunteering myself to be Your arms, Your feet, Your hands to hurting and needy people. I want to embrace Your heart for the poor, the orphan, and the widow. I want to offer to You the field You have given me, that You would show me how to help provide for those who are less fortunate. Lord, I ask You to speak to me. Lead me into the avenues of service that I am to engage in. Lord, according to James 1:5, give me the wisdom I need to move forward and to connect with the right people. Today I make a commitment in my heart, with my mouth, to show You and the world my faith, by my works—because I love You and I know that You love me. In Jesus' name, amen.

AFTERWORD

The three books in the Women on the Frontlines series—*A Call to Courage, A Call to the Secret Place,* and *A Call to Compassion*—are not just a history tour of great women of God. These books encompass the life journey of a person whose shadow is yet being cast to this day.

First, these books are about the transforming power of the Lord Jesus Christ Himself. None of these women, Michal Ann Willard Goll included, could have made the difference they did without the Son of God, Jesus Christ the Lord, sacrificing His life for us. If you do not know this amazing Savior, then the first thing to do is give your heart to Him. Give your life to Him, as He has already given His best for you.

Second, these books are about the transforming power of the Holy Spirit in lives today. At the time of this writing, Michal Ann has already been worshipping the Lord unabated before His throne for several years. Someday I will join my dear Annie on the other side. I trust you will as well. It will be grand!

But "grand" does not wait till the other side. It is not the length of our days but the depth of our impact that matters. With this eternal life view in mind, I want to give you my own call—*A Call to Do What Matters.* Whether it is to be a man or woman of courage, the secret place, or compassion, just do what matters most. Love God. Love your family. Love your neighbor. Love the world that Jesus died for. Just do it!

The Origins of Compassion Acts and Women on the Frontlines

Compassion Acts first began as a good intention, like most good ideas. However, what made the difference was the woman behind the thought, Michal Ann Goll. She took her good intention of making a difference in the world, and did just that. After she spent months in prayer, seeking clarity on the direction for her ideas, she began networking with friends, and friends of friends.

Through these connections and strong convictions, Compassion Acts was birthed in 2004 as a ministry and humanitarian aid organization to provide help for those in need. Long before this, Michal Ann and I together had started a yearly conference known as Women on the Frontlines. We originally held the conferences in Nashville, Tennessee (the buckle of the Bible Belt), and later we took them elsewhere within the Ohio and Tennessee Valleys. We did this together for eleven years. After her death, I chaired the twelfth year myself.

Passing of Batons—Forward Motion

I then turned to our dear friend, Patricia King of XP Media, and asked her to be the co-chair with me for Women on the Frontlines for the thirteenth year. It was a great fit. Eventually I felt the direction of the Lord to release and empower Patricia to be the international director of Women on the Frontlines and she accepted. Since that time, these gatherings have turned into a global movement (see woflglobal.com). The Lord knows what He is doing, and I am grateful.

Michal Ann founded Compassion Acts, and affected thousands of individuals herself. However, Michal Ann passed away the morning of September 15, 2008, after a five-year battle with colon cancer. Even though she is no longer with us today, we still carry on the heart and soul of Compassion Acts in her stead. In turn, I recognized Mark Roye, Michal Ann's assistant, to become the international director of Compassion Acts. This too has been a wise choice, as Mark loves Jesus and the poor of the earth. To learn more, please see the last page in this book.

Today, Compassion Acts operates in a pursuit of justice, disaster relief, and humanitarian aid work in response to Michal Ann's personal charge found in her last will and testament:

> It has been my goal and desire to love the Lord with all my heart all the days of my life. My desire is to leave with my family, friends and ministry partners a challenge to always love and honor God with all your life. I request that you not forget the poor that Jesus died for and that you carry on my ministry of Compassion Acts to the world.

> Michal Ann Goll (handwritten on February 4, 2008)

Now It's Your Turn

I now invite you to be a man or woman on the front lines and make a difference for such a time as this. I challenge you to take up the baton and love God with all your heart, soul, and strength. And along with the great cloud of witnesses, I make a request of you: Do not forget the poor that Jesus died for, and carry on this vibrant ministry of Compassion Acts to the world. Does our Father in heaven deserve anything less?

As a small token of commitment, I am dedicating the royalties of this book, *A Call to Compassion,* to the ongoing work of Compassion Acts. Your mere purchase of this book has already made a difference in someone's life, and I thank you for that.

Always remember—together, in Jesus, we make a great team!

ABOUT THE AUTHORS

DR. JAMES W. GOLL is the founder of Encounters Network, Prayer Storm, and the God Encounters Training eSchool. James in an international bestselling author, a certified Life Language Trainer, and has taught in more than fifty nations. James was married to Michal Ann for thirty-two years before her graduation to heaven in the fall of 2008. James has four adult children who are married and a growing number of grandchildren. James makes his home in Franklin, Tennessee.

MICHAL ANN GOLL was a lover of Jesus all her life, the devoted wife of James Goll for thirty-two years, and mother of four beloved children. She was the founder of Compassion Acts, a member of the Debra Company Founder's Group, and honored to be listed in the Cambridge Who's Who. She traveled the globe demonstrating that love takes action. She authored eight books and co-established the Women on the Frontlines conferences. She graduated to her heavenly reward in the fall of 2008 and is greatly missed to this day by thousands of people around the world.

EncountersNetwork.com
PO Box 1653, Franklin, TN 37065
info@encountersnetwork.com
615-599-5552 | 877-200-1604

ACKNOWLEDGMENTS

We would like to thank all those who made *A Call to Compassion* come to pass. An enormous thank-you goes to the original publisher, Destiny Image, for seeing it as worthy to be published. BroadStreet Publishing came along later and dusted off this treasure to present it in a new format. Thank you to both publishing houses for your dedication.

Michal Ann was in the beginning stages of her fight with cancer when this project began. Therefore, out of all three of these books, this last book was a definite group effort. It would not have happened without the contributions of Mallory Gabard, Lloyd Hildebrand, Julia Loren, Don Milam, Dr. J. Mark Rodgers, Ada Winn, Kathy Deering, David Sluka, and possibly several others. How wonderful it is to have had a whole company of dedicated believers work together to get this strategic message out.

Then there's the Compassion Acts team. We wish to acknowledge and thank Mark Roye, GraceAnn Goll Visser, Leon Hoover, Dabney Mann, Marcus Young, Kay Durham, Mike and Sisse Phieffer, Ann Bell, Marion Farrar, Justin Goll, all the interns, and those who partnered to see Michal Ann's dream come to pass—and continue to this day. Many thanks also to all the prayer warriors who continually lifted us up in prayer. You have been the guardians, watching over this little baby named Compassion Acts. You have created a safe place for the birth of this message and ministry.

In closing, here is Michal Ann's original statement of acknowledgment: "Most importantly, oh my dear Jesus—thank you for waking me up, and not letting me stay enclosed in my own little world. Thank you for expanding my vision, my dreams, my goals, and my heart."

NOTES

Chapter 1: God's Heart of Compassion

1. David Ruis, *The Justice God Is Seeking* (Ventura, CA: Regal Books, 2006), 80.

2. Ibid., 10.

3. From Charles H. Spurgeon, "The Compassion of Jesus," sermon delivered at the Metropolitan Tabernacle, Newington, England.

4. Ruis.

Chapter 2: The Compassionate Power of Tears

1. John Wimber and Kevin Springer, *Power Healing* (San Francisco: HarperCollins, 1987), 47–48.

2. Dick Eastman, *No Easy Road* (Grand Rapids, MI: Baker Books, 1971), 92.

3. From Richard Foster, *Prayer: Finding the Heart's True Home* (New York: HarperCollins, 1992), 39–40.

4. Ibid., 37–38.

5. Eastman, 93.

Chapter 3: The Mother of the Salvation Army

1. "Catherine Booth" (http://spartacus-educational.com/Wbooth.htm). Many of the details in this chapter come from this article.

2. Ibid.

3. Ibid.

4. Ibid.

5. Ibid.

7. Vinita Hampton Wright and Mary Horner Collins, *Women's Wisdom Through the Ages* (Wheaton, IL: Harold Shaw, 1994), 69.

8. "Catherine Booth." (Spartacus. schoolnet.co.uk).

9. Helen K. Hosier, *William and Catherine Booth: Founders of the Salvation Army: Heroes of the Faith* (Uhrichsville, OH: Barbour Publishing, 1999), 58.

10. Ibid., 76–77.

11. "Catherine Booth." (http://spartacus-educational.com/Wbooth.htm)

Chapter 4: Beloved Woman of the Cherokee

1. Pat Aldenman, *Nancy Ward/Dragging Canoe* (Johnson City, TN: The Overmountain Press, 1990). Very little is written about Nancy Ward, and this is one of the only sources. The Cherokee Nation's history, though, is well documented. The author of this chapter, Ada Winn, is a descendant of Nancy Ward.

Chapter 5: The Lady with the Lamp

1. Basil Miller, *Florence Nightingale: The Lady of the Lamp (Women of Faith)* (Bethany House, 1975), 72.

2. Sam Wellman, *Florence Nightingale: Lady with the Lamp: (Heroes of the Faith)* (Uhrichsville, OH: Barbour Publishing, 1999), 58.

3. Mary Ford-Grabowsky, ed., *Sacred Voices: Essential Women's Wisdom Through the Ages* (San Francisco: HarperCollins, 2002), 128.

4. Wellman, 98.

5. Ibid., 123–127.

6. Ibid., 127.

7. Ibid., 140.

8. Ibid., 152–153.

9. Ibid., 156.

10. Ibid., 168–169.

11. Ibid., 169.

12. Ibid., 166.

13. James E. Keifer, "Florence Nightingale, Nurse, Renewer of Society," *Biographical Sketches* (http://justus.anglican.org/resources/bio/158.html).

14. Muhammad Umair Mushtaq, "Public Health in British India: A Brief Account of the History of Medical Services and Disease Prevention in

Colonial India," *Indian Journal of Community Medicine* 2009 Jan; 34(1): 6–14. (http://www.ncbi.nlm. nih.gov/pmc/articles/PMC2763662/).

15. Kiefer.

16. Ibid., 202.

Chapter 6: Rejected by Man, Approved by God

1. Janet and Geoff Benge, *Gladys Aylward: The Adventure of a Lifetime, (Christian Heroes: Then & Now)* (YWAM Publishers, 1998), 170.

2. Ibid., 20–21.

3. Gladys Aylward (as told to Christine Hunter) *Gladys Aylward: The Little Woman* (Chicago: Moody Publishers, 1974), 10–12.

4. Benge, 33.

5. Sam Wellman, *Gladys Aylward: Missionary to China (Heroes of the Faith)* (Uhrichsville, OH: Barbour Publishing, 1998), 34.

6. Aylward, 31.

7. Ibid., 42.

8. Benge, 104.

9. Ibid., 169.

10. Ibid., 201.

Chapter 7: The Humble Road

1. Eileen Egan and Kathleen Egan, OSB, eds., *Suffering Into Joy* (Ann Arbor, MI: Servant Publications, 1994), 13.

2. Egan, 21.

3. Nobelprize.org, "Mother Teresa: Biographical" (http://www. nobelprize.org/nobel_prizes/peace/ laureates/1979/teresa-bio.html).

4. Words of acceptance for the Nobel Peace Prize, from "Mother Teresa: In Her Own Words," The Associated Press, September 5, 1997, in the archives of the *Washington Post* (https://www.washingtonpost.com/ wp-srv/inatl/longterm/teresa/stories/ words.htm).

6. John Paul II, "Address of John Paul II to the Pilgrims Who Had Come to Rome for the Beatification of Mother Teresa," 2003.

7. Benedict XVI, *Deus Caritas Est.*

8. Egan and Egan, 14.

9. Ibid., 22.

10. Ibid., 32–33.

11. Nobelprize.org, "Mother Teresa: Lecture" (http://nobelprize.org/peace/ laureates/1979/teresa-lecture.html).

12. Mother Teresa, "Whatsoever you do…" speech to National Prayer Breakfast (http://www.priestsforlife. org/mother-teresa/breakfast-letter.htm).

13. T. T. Mundakel, *Blessed Mother Teresa: Her Journey to Your Heart,* English trans. ed. (Liguori, MO: Liguori Publications, 2003), n.p.

14. Egan, 140–141.

15. Ibid., 65.

Chapter 8: Little Women, Big God

1. Amy Carmichael, Gold Cord (Fort Washington, PA: Christian Literature Crusade, 1932, 1996), n.p.

2. Ibid.

3. Ibid.

4. "Carmichael, Amy (1867–1951), Gospel Fellowship Association (https://www.gfamissions.org/ missionary-biographies/carmichael- amy-1867-1951.html).

5. Frank L. Houghton, Amy Carmichael of Dohnavur: The Story of a Lover and her Beloved (Fort Washington, PA: Christian Literature Crusade, 1953, 1979), n.p.

6. Ibid.

7. Amy Carmichael, Thou Givest… They Gather (Fort Washington, PA: Christian Literature Crusade, 1958, 1971), 134.

8. "Mother Katharine Drexel could be the second American canonized saint born in the United States," Catholic World News, as reported in DailyCatholic.org, January 22—24, 1999, Section Three, vol. 10, no. 15. (http://www.dailycatholic.org/issue /archives/1999Jan/15jan22,vol.10, no.15txt/jan22dc3.htm).

9. Ibid.

10. Ibid.

11. Vatican News Service, "Katharine Drexel (1858–1955)" (http://www.vatican.va/news_services/liturgy/saints/ns_lit_doc_20001001_katharine-drexel_en.html).

12. From the 1907 Constitutions of the Congregation of the Blessed Sacrament for Indians and Colored People.

13. Vatican News Service.

14. Barbara Howie, "Phoebe Palmer (1807–1874)" West Virginia University (http://are.as.wvu.edu/phebe.htm).

15. Rev. Richard Wheatley, The Life and Letters of Mrs. Phoebe Palmer (New York: Palmer and Hughes, 1876), 18.

16. Ibid., 26.

17. Howie.

18. Ibid.

19. Ibid.

20. Tommy Tenney, Mary's Prayers and Martha's Recipes (Shippensburg, PA: Destiny Image, 2002).

21. Ibid.Bridget Hill, Women Alone: Spinsters in England, 1660–1850 (New Haven, CT: Yale University Press, 2001), 156.

22. Tenney, 18.

23. Tryon Edwards, ed., A Dictionary of Thoughts (Detroit, MI: F.B Dickerson, 1908), 431.

24. Ibid., 540.

25. Angela Bull, Elizabeth Fry (Newton Abbot, England: David and Charles, 1988), 23.

26. Ibid.

27. Ibid.

28. Richard Huntsman, Elizabeth Fry: Quaker and Prison Reformer (Guist Bottom, Dereham, Norfolk, UK: Larks Press, 1998), 3.

29. Ibid., 27.

30. Ibid., 52.

31. Ibid.

Chapter 9: Blessed Are the Poor

1. Lee Grady, "Heidi Baker's Uncomfortable Message to America," Charisma magazine, August 2006.

2. Ibid.

3. Julia Loren, Shifting Shadows of Supernatural Power (Shippensburg, PA: Destiny Image, 2006), 91.

4. Rolland and Heidi Baker, There Is Always Enough (Grand Rapids, MI: Chosen Books, 2002), 26.

5. C. Hope Flinchbaugh, "Brave Hearts in a Desperate Land," Charisma magazine, March 2006.

6. Josie Newman, "Miracles and Church Growth Mark Mozambique Ministry," Charisma magazine, March 2004.

7. Baker and Baker, 160.

8. Ibid., 67–68.

9. Ibid., 68–69.

10. Loren, 108.

11. Flinchbaugh, Charisma, March 2006.

12. Baker and Baker, 176–177.

13. John Crowder, Miracle Workers, Reformers, and The New Mystics (Shippensburg, PA: Destiny Image, 2006), 147.

Chapter 10: It's Got to Be Personal

1. Sharon Salzberg, "The Power of Intention," O Magazine, January 2004.

2. Mahesh Chavda, Only Love Can Make a Miracle (Ann Arbor, MI: Servant, 1990), 72–73.

3. Ken Blue, The Authority to Heal (Downers Grove, IL: InterVarsity Press, 1987).

4. John Wimber and Kevin Springer, Power Healing (San Francisco, CA: HarperCollins, 1987), 47–48.

Chapter 11: Compassion Acts

1. Charles Spurgeon, sermon #3438, "The Compassion of Jesus," The Spurgeon Archive (http://www.spurgeon.org/sermons/3438.htm).

2. Ibid., 165–168.

3. Human Rights Watch, "Burma: World's Highest Number of Child Soldiers," October 16, 2002 (http://www.hrw.org/press/2002/10/burma-1016.htm).

COMPASSION ACTS
love taking action

Compassion Acts was founded by Michal Ann Goll in 2004 as a ministry and humanitarian aid organization to provide help for those in need. Even though she is no longer with us today, we still carry on the heart and soul of Compassion Acts in her stead.

Today, Compassion Acts operates in a pursuit of justice, disaster relief and humanitarian aid work in response to Michal Ann's personal charge found in her last will and testament.

CA EFFORTS AROUND THE WORLD

Mission Projects -
sending resources and volunteers to help meet specific needs

Emergency Relief -
responding to natural disasters through rice shipments and humanitarian aid

Project Dreamers Park -
building playgrounds and community centers to inspire children to dream

First Nations in America -
serving Native Americans by providing food, health supplies and education

Want to Get Involved? Find out More at:
CAMPASSIONACTS.COM